There are lots more ideas where these came from.

This book is only one of an entire library of **Ideas** volumes that are available from Youth Specialties. Each volume is completely different and contains tons of tried and tested programming ideas submitted by the world's most creative youth workers. Order the others by using the form below.

Combo Books

52 volumes of **Ideas** have been updated and republished in four-volume combinations. For example, our combo book **Ideas 1-4** is actually four books in one—volumes 1 through 4. These combos are a bargain at $19.95 each (that's 50% off!).

The Entire Library

The **Ideas** Library includes every volume and an index to volumes 1-52. See the form below for the current price, or call the Youth Specialties Order Center at 800/776-8008.

SAVE UP TO 50%!

IDEAS ORDER FORM (or call 800/776-8008)

Your Idea May Be Worth $100

It's worth at least $25 if we publish it in a future volume of **Ideas**. And it's worth $100 if it's chosen as the outstanding idea of the book it appears in.

It's not really a contest, though—just our way of saying thanks for sharing your creativity with us. If you have a good idea that worked well with your group, send it in. We'll look it over and decide whether or not we can include it in a future **Ideas** book. If we do, we'll send you at least 25 bucks!

In addition to that, the **Ideas** editor will select one especially creative idea from each new book as the outstanding idea of that particular book—and send a check for $100 to its contributor.

So don't let your good ideas go to waste. Write them down and send them to us, accompanied by this form. Explain your ideas completely (without getting ridiculous) and include illustrations, diagrams, photos, samples, or any other materials you think are helpful.

FILL OUT BELOW

Name _____

Address_____

City _____ State __ Zip _____

Phone (_____) _____

Write or type your idea(s) (one idea per sheet) and attach it to this form or to a copy of this form. Include your name and address with each idea you send. Mail to Ideas, 1224 Greenfield Drive, El Cajon, CA 92021. Ideas submitted to Youth Specialties cannot be returned.

IDEAS • 54

CONTENTS

CROWD BREAKERS

Label Laughs

Sheets of computer labels and marking pens are all you need for these two crowd breakers.

➤ **Tattoo.** This easy mixer doubles as a reminder that individual identities make a church body strong. Each player writes his or her own name on each label on the sheet. On a signal, kids begin to "tattoo" everyone else in the room with their labels. Players must introduce themselves to others before tattooing them.

The first person to run out of labels is the winner. A second winner is the one who *collects* the most labels. Before everyone removes their tattoos, ask them to review the names they are stuck with.

➤ **Sticky Signatures**. In this variation, Allison (a fictitious player) must fill her sheet of labels with the signatures of others. After signing one of Allison's labels, the signer then detaches it from the sheet and sticks it on Allison's elbow, palm, nose—anywhere on her body that isn't already covered by a label (within the bounds of good taste, of course). Give a prize to the person whose body is covered with the most signatures within a time limit.

Pat McGlone, Savannah, Ga., and Becky R. Ker, Paris, Ont., Canada

Bumpy Brain

To perform this "magic" stunt, choose one student to be your assistant—and tell her beforehand how the trick is done.

Your group thinks of a number between 1 and 10; someone in the group whispers the number to your assistant. Announce that you will use your expert skill to tell them *the number they chose* by feeling the bumps on your assistant's skull.

Place both of your hands on your assistant's head—your thumbs on her jawbones near her ears—and pretend to feel the bumps on her skull for a few seconds. What you're actually feeling, however, is how many times your assistant clenches her jaws, which you can feel with your thumbs. Astound your group by declaring the very number they selected! *Les Christie, Fullerton, Calif.*

Computer Spellcheck

When spellcheck tags a mispelled word in a computer document, it probably suggests alternative spellings to replace the original word you used.

So have some fun: spellchecking proper names produces some hilarious substitutions (which are, on occasion, strangely accurate). The name Duffy Robbins, for instance, brings up Puffy Robbing. Tony Campolo becomes Tony Carpool. The contributor of this idea becomes Ralph Realigned, Reloaned, or Reliant.

Ask the computer buffs in your group to run the youth directory through spellcheck, then choose the funniest alternative names and write them on name tags to use at the next youth activity. Kids who arrive must first of all find their own name tags; then they all can vote for the most outrageous name, the most accurate description generated by the computer, etc.

Students with winning names receive awards.

Ralph Rowland, Bellevue, Wash.

Crazy School Daze Mixer

For this September get-acquainted game, give each student a copy of page 9. The first player to have all assignments initialed wins. *Tom Lytle, Marion, Ohio*

Crazy School Daze

1. Find four people who don't go to your school, then form a train (hands on shoulders of the person in front of you) in grade order, and cruise around the room reciting the Pledge of Allegiance. Have each member of your train initial here:

_____ _____ _____ _____

2. Remember the Rock-Paper-Scissors game? Find a partner to play Teacher-Principal-Parent. Stand back to back, count to three, then quickly turn around in the pose of a teacher (a "Thinker" pose—chin on fist), a principal (hands on hips, scowling), or a parent (shaking a finger in the partner's face). Teacher beats a parent, parent beats a principal, principal beats a teacher. The loser initials winner's sheet here:

_____

(Loser must play with different people until he or she wins.)

3. Find two other people. Lay on the floor, form the letter F and yell, "I should have studied more!" Have the other two people initial here:

_____ _____

4. Find someone of the opposite sex. Each of you add up the total number of letters in your first, middle, and last names. The person with the longest name gets his or her paper initialed here by the loser: _____ *(If you tie, you both win. If you lose, play with different people until you win.)*

5. Time for P.E.! Find three other people and play leapfrog. Everyone in your group must jump at least once. Have the two other frogs initial here:

_____ _____

6. Find someone for a match of Toe Fencing (face another player, clasp hands, and try to tap the top of your opponent's foot with your foot)— freshmen play juniors, sophomores play seniors. The first person to "strike" wins. If you win, the loser initials here:

_____

(If you lose, play twice more with different people; if you still lose, initial your own paper.)

CHAPTER TWO

GAMES

Safecracker II

On a safe or trunk is a locked padlock—the kind with 39 numbers on it. The object is to crack the combination and get the prize in the safe—a discount coupon to your next retreat, a free teen devotional book, tickets to a concert, etc.

To find the combination, students comb the building or playing field for the number of objects listed on the sheet—then eliminate those numbers. *John McLendon, Hendersonville, Tenn.*

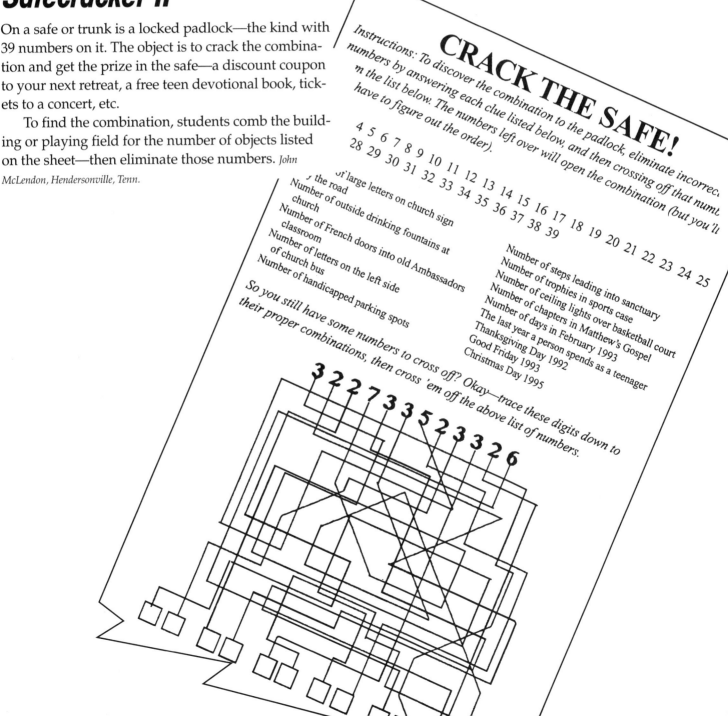

CRACK THE SAFE!

Instructions: To discover the combination to the padlock, eliminate incorrec... numbers by answering each clue listed below, and then crossing off that num... m the list below. The numbers left over will open the combination (but you'll have to figure out the order).

4 5 6 7 8 9 10 11 12 13 14 15 16 17 18 19 20 21 22 23 24 25
28 29 30 31 32 33 34 35 36 37 38 39

...f large letters on church sign
...y the road
Number of outside drinking fountains at church
Number of French doors into old Ambassadors classroom
Number of letters on the left side of church bus
Number of handicapped parking spots

Number of steps leading into sanctuary
Number of trophies in sports case
Number of ceiling lights over basketball court
Number of chapters in Matthew's Gospel
The last year a person spends as a teenager
Thanksgiving Day 1992
Good Friday 1993
Christmas Day 1995

So you still have some numbers to cross off? Okay—trace these digits down to their proper combinations, then cross 'em off the above list of numbers.

3 2 2 7 3 3 5 2 3 3 2 6

Spaghetti Relay

This is a variation on the good ol' Life Saver-on-a-toothpick relay: uncooked spaghetti instead of Life Savers, and straws instead of toothpicks.

Divide your group into relay teams of any size and give each player a nonbendable drinking straw. Players fold the end of their straws (about an inch from the end, so the spaghetti won't be inhaled or become soggy from saliva) and then grip the straws in their teeth.

Start the relay by placing a whole piece of uncooked spaghetti into the straw of the first person. Without using hands, that person must slide the spaghetti into the next person's straw, etc., until they reach the end of the line. Then, the last person must run to the front of the line as soon as possible.

If a piece of spaghetti drops, the person in the front must start the whole process over again with a new length of spaghetti. *Greg Miller, Knoxville, Tenn.*

Strategic Capture the Flag

This is Capture the Flag (*Ideas 1*), but on steroids. Water makes the game a blast, and the strategic aspect makes your kids work together as a team.

All players tuck a sock, bandanna, or rag into their waistbands. As in traditional Capture the Flag, players are captured when their sock is taken in enemy territory. Captured players are then imprisoned, how and where you and the kids decide.

Here are the twists that make Strategic Capture the Flag the high-powered game it is:

➤ **Safety zone.** Each team creates a safety zone—with a 10-foot circle of rope—around their flag. No one can be taken prison while inside this rope.

➤ **Gun emplacement.** Inside another 10-foot loop of rope, anywhere in the team's home turf, is a trash can full of water balloons. This is the team's "gun emplacement"—the only site from which water balloons may be thrown. Getting hit with a water balloon makes you a prisoner just as having your sock taken—except that such liquid shelling is effective anywhere, even on the enemy's own turf.

➤ **Tanks.** Each team also has two "tanks"—each one consists of two people, one riding piggyback on the other. The one on top has a plastic pitcher of water. Getting doused by a tank makes you a prisoner. Just remember two points: tanks can take prisoners any-

where (on friendly or enemy territory) and only a tank can take another tank prisoner.

Make sure each team has a plentiful supply of water for their tanks, or have them agree on a neutral faucet. And use plenty of referees to avoid inventive rule bending.

Give each team plenty of prep time to make a strategy. You may want to play several shorter games instead of one long one; this gives each team a chance to try different strategies. *John Young, Philadelphia, Pa.*

Tabloid Game

The object of this game is to distinguish between actual and contrived tabloid headlines.

1. Purchase several supermarket tabloids, skim them, and write the best headlines on index cards (one headline per card). Write up 10 to 20 of them.

2. Label the back of each card with a letter—A, B, C, etc.

3. Now compose some tabloid-type headlines of your own—write twice as many fakes as you have actual headlines. (Recruit a few students or sponsors to help you write the bogus headlines.) Keep a master list of correct headlines for yourself or the emcee.

4. On the backs of two fake headlines cards, write the letter A; on the backs of another two fakes, write

B; etc. What you're doing is making triads: each triad has an actual tabloid headline and two made-up ones.

5. To start the game, choose three youth "panelists" (perhaps the ones who helped you write the headlines); each of them will read one of the three cards in a triad.

6. Divide the other students into teams of three to eight or so, depending on the size of your group.

7. Give an A card to each of the three panelists. Each panelist reads the headline on his or her index card.

8. Allow a minute for teams to confer and guess which of the three headlines is the actual one. Award points to each team guessing the correct headline.

Or you can buy Tabloids, the commercial form of the same game (Pressman, about $25). *David A. Narigon, Washington, Pa.*

Triangle Tag

Have kids gather into groups of four. Three of them should form a triangle by holding hands or wrists. The fourth person stands in the middle of the triangle.

Choose one group to be "It." A successful tag occurs only when the person in the middle of a triangle tags *another* middler. The trick, of course, is for the triangle to track with their middler, to anticipate his or her direction and strategy—or at least to hear the middler's verbal instructions. The other groups, of course, try to avoid being tagged while staying inside the boundaries.

Every few games rotate members within their group, so everyone gets a turn inside the triangle. (Besides being fun, "Triangle Tag" can effectively introduce sessions about submission, humility, and cooperation.) *Alan Rathbun, Harrisburg, Pa.*

Prison Ball

The more players, the better for this classic game that is played indoors best (where walls are the court's boundaries), but a playground version works okay, too. You'll need one, two, or three playground balls (depending on the size of your group). Divide your group into two equal teams—we'll call them Reds and Whites, for the sake of the diagram below.

The game begins with each team on their half of

the court, and each team with at least one ball (unless the group is small—10 on side, say. In this case, use a single ball). Now for the rules:

➤ The object is to send all of your opponents to prison.

➤ You send opponents to prison by hitting them with the ball.

➤ Opponents who *catch* the ball, however, stay free and don't go to prison.

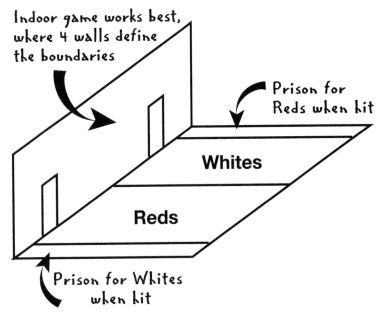

Indoor game works best, where 4 walls define the boundaries

Prison for Reds when hit

Whites

Reds

Prison for Whites when hit

➤ Players in prison regain their freedom by hitting an opponent with the ball.

➤ Prisoners get a ball either by one slipping through their opponent's half of the court, or by their still-free teammates lobbing balls deliberately to their comrades in prison.

➤ You must stay on your side of the middle line.

➤ You may not step into the prison behind your half of the court.

Teenagers can throw balls *hard*, so make rules appropriate to your group. Possible variations: balls must hit players below the waist (or thrower goes to prison)...use soft, mushy Nerf-type balls...boys hit boys, girls hit girls (just make sure there are equal numbers on each side)...etc. *Christopher Graham, Santa Barbara, Calif.*

Volleypit

First make The Pit: set tables with fold-up legs on their sides, like this:

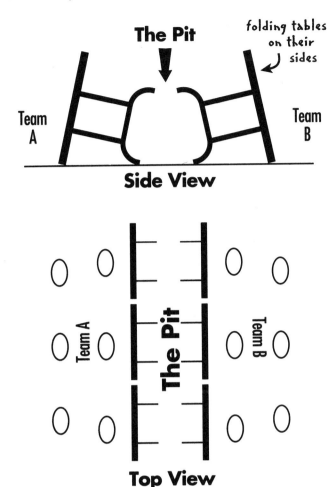

The Pit

folding tables on their sides

Team A

Team B

Side View

Team A

The Pit

Team B

Top View

Now you divide players into two teams (6-10 on a team, depending on room size) and play volleyball the normal way, though with a volleyball-sized, *very light* foam ball (even hard-surfaced Nerf Balls may be too heavy). The Pit is the "net"—but woe to the players who hit the ball into The Pit instead of over it! For they go into The Pit themselves—and stay there, without obstructing play, until a player from the opposing team Pits the ball.

If more than one player from a team wind up in The Pit, they return to their team in the order they went into The Pit. You win one of two ways: by scoring the traditional 15 points, or if all a team's players end up in The Pit.

Variation: Paddlepit, played with a smaller, softball-sized Nerf Ball and Smashball-type paddles.

Greg Hughes, Chillicothe, Mo.

Wrong Way Baseball

This is an indoor or outdoor version of baseball, depending on the size of the group and your facilities. Play follows the standard rules, except that alternating batters run opposite directions around the bases when they get a hit.

For instance, say Batter 1 gets a hit, so she runs as usual to first base on a single. Then say Batter 2 gets a hit; he runs the opposite way—to *third* base—and so clockwise around the diamond. The catch, of course, is when two base runners are approaching the same base from different directions. If both arrive on the same base at the end of a play, they're both out.

Hilarious antics follow when kids realize they haven't thought ahead to what may happen next if they continue their course without cooperation. The team in the field must also talk to each other more to keep up with where the best plays are. (Do we smell a teachable moment here?)

Some details about "Wrong Way Baseball":
➤ A hitter who runs the wrong direction must first return to and touch home plate before running to the appropriate base.
➤ The direction hitters run is based on *batting* order, not hitting order. In other words, odd-numbered batters (not hitters) run the bases normally; even numbered batters, if they get a hit, run the bases clockwise.
➤ In a gymnasium or large room, use a Whiffle Ball and bat. Fly balls caught after ricocheting off a wall or ceiling are not outs.

Kent Taylor, Redford, Va.

Wireless Sardines

This variation of "Sardines" (*Ideas 18*) uses a wireless microphone. "It" takes the microphone and hides within range of the sound system. The rest of the group waits for "It" to give clues about where she's hiding.

If one in the group suspects "Its" location, he tries to track her down. If he fails to find "It," he returns to the sanctuary to wait for another clue. "It" gives a new clue every 30 to 40 seconds. Whoever finds "It" hides with her (as in "Sardines"). The last one to find "It" (or the first one) is the next to hide. (For an extended "Sardine" event, see "Vehicular Sardines" on page 29.) *Scott C. McLeod, Manchester, Conn.*

Wally Pong

The table tennis version of Wallyball, Wally Pong is best played in a small room with high ceilings (but any room is adequate).

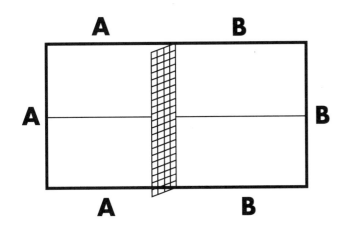

Place a Ping-Pong table in the center of the room and put three players on each side. Then play and score like volleyball:

➤ Upon receiving the serve, players don't try to immediately return the ball, but instead set the ball for teammates.
➤ Three hits per side.
➤ Slams (or spikes) are acceptable.
➤ The ball is in play until it hits the floor.
➤ Shots off walls, ceilings, people, etc., are playable.
➤ A team holds the service as long as it scores.
➤ Servers rotate.
➤ 15 points win the game.

Mike Vickers, Valley, Ala.

Mix 'Em Up

This variation on musical chairs works best with at least 15 players—the more the merrier. Set up a circle of chairs, one for each player except the leader. All the players sit down.

The leader calls out a random characteristic present in the group—"Everyone with purple socks!" All players who share that characteristic get up and scramble for new seats vacated by other players doing the same thing. The leader also darts for a seat. When the seats are filled, one player is left standing—who chooses the next characteristic, and so on.

If absolutely *nothing* comes to mind, "It" can always say, "Mix 'em up!" at which all players get up and find new seats. *Christopher Graham, Santa Barbara, Calif.*

Scrabble Scramble

Give several sheets of construction paper and markers to each of two or more equal-numbered teams. Assign each team a word, one letter per team member. Then the kids write one letter per sheet of paper in large bold print for all to see easily.

The object of the game is to stump the other teams. For example, members of a team that is assigned the word *Nazareth* may stand up and hold their letters in this order:

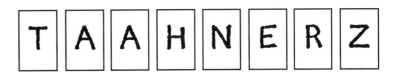

The team that guesses the correct word in the shortest time wins the round.

"Scrabble Scramble" is easily adapted to any topical, biblical, or seasonal lesson or study by simply using words that are pertinent to the topic, passage, or season.

Or try this variation:

1. Beforehand, write out the letters of a word (or short phrase) on separate sheets of paper. Make as many sets of the word as there are teams.

2. Shuffle the letters in each set so they're out of order.

3. At the meeting, give a set of scrambled letters to each team.

4. On a signal each team tries to be the first to unscramble the word, each player lining up in order with his or her letter.

Michael Capps, East Flat Rock, N.C.

Winter Olympics II

Host an indoor Winter Olympics with these sports:

➤ **The Biathlon.** Make cross-country skis for indoor use with some cardboard and masking tape. Just cut long strips of cardboard for the skis, and tape an old pair of shoes to them for the boots. Then set up your course with three or so shooting stations along the way. Arm your biathletes with water guns; at each station sits one of their teammates, lit candle in mouth. The biathlete shoots out the candle, skis on to repeat the process at the next stations, then skis to the finish.

➤ **The Downhill Slalom.** This is a wonderful event if you have access to a long staircase. Make slalom gates out of short dowels with construction paper hung on one end to look like a flag. Tape these onto the stair railing so the flags hang into the path of the downhiller—like this:

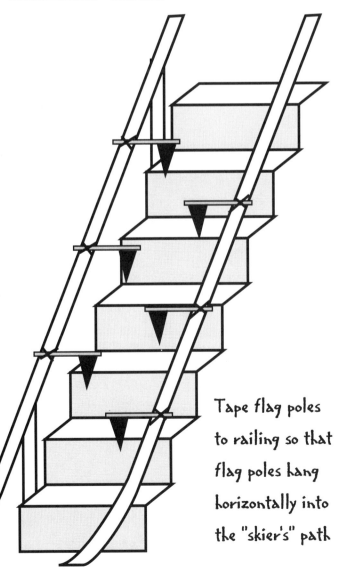

Tape flag poles to railing so that flag poles hang horizontally into the "skier's" path

To discourage kids from racing down the stairs and breaking their necks, don't make this a timed event. Instead, let the challenge be for each skier to ski down the stairs with a mouthful of water, which goes into an empty bucket at the bottom. The team to reach the bottom with the most water is declared the winner.

➤ **The Ski Jump.** In this initiative problem, give each team a Ping-Pong ball (with a picture of a skier drawn on it), a piece of poster board, and a roll of Scotch tape. Each team must develop the best way to propel their "skier" the farthest distance. And just so it's legal to call it "Ski Jump," give them a ski to jump: in order for it to be a legal jump, the skier must at least make the length of the ski.

For *outdoor* games (brrr!), see "Winter Olympics" in *Ideas 24*. *Pat McGlone, Savannah, Ga..*

A to Z Scavenger Hunt

Each of your five or six teams needs a vehicle as well as a responsible, licensed driver. Determine at what time each team must return to the starting point. The goal: to collect evidence from 26 shops and stores they visit—one store for each letter of the alphabet (*A*rby's, *B*lockbuster Video, *C*loth World, etc.).

Details of this hunt:
➤ Each letter is given a random point value before the teams venture out.
➤ Letters such as Q or Z should be assigned a higher value than the more common letters (such as A or T), since they might be more difficult to locate.
➤ Evidence from the stores can be a business card, a bag imprinted with the business's name, a matchbook, etc.

Upon their return, teams total their scores and a winner is declared. Deduct one point for every minute a team is delayed beyond the time limit.
Cheryl Ehlers, East Point, Ga.

Video Sound Effects

Before your party or event, videotape several objects that operate or run with distinctive sounds—a train, race car, photocopier, typewriter or keyboard, the youth-room door shutting, voices of individuals in your congregation, etc. Make sure the camcorder's microphone picks up the audio.

At the event, conceal the TV screen with a piece of cardboard and pass out pencils and slips of paper. Then play the tape, so that kids hear only the *sounds* of the operations you recorded. Pause between each sound so students can write down their guesses as to what produced that sound. When they're done, rewind the tape, remove the cardboard from the TV screen, and replay the tape, letting kids see *and* hear it this time. The student who identified the most sounds wins. *Len Cuthbert, Hamilton, Ont., Canada*

Bungee Running

For this boomerang foot race, borrow six or more bungee-jumping harnesses and bungee cords that allow for the different weights of your students. Anchor several bungee cords to something immovable, strap in as many willing teenagers, line them up, and say "Go!" Whoever runs *farthest* wins. Mark the winning distance with a Frisbee so the following sprinters have a visual goal to strive for. *Steve Duyst, Tulare, Calif.*

Whistle Sprint

Have some teenagers in your group who are full of hot air? Give each student a playing card and a whistle (cheap plastic whistles work great). On a starting line, line up teenagers (on their knees, whistles in mouths) and their cards (on the ground in front of them), point out the finish line, and let 'em go! Players must blow their cards—"through" their whistles—to the finish line.

If the noise gets to you, you can always replace the whistles with straws. *Rob Ely, St. Albans, W.Va.*

Whiffle Hockey

For indoor or outdoor fun, create your own hockey sticks and play with a Wiffle Ball. You'll need a Wiffle Ball, several old broom sticks, empty two-liter plastic soda bottles, and duct tape. Screw the broom sticks into the soda bottles and tape to secure.

Follow normal hockey rules, or make up your own. Variations can increase the fun—wear rollerblades while playing, or replace the Whiffle Ball with a thick-skinned balloon. *Keith Curran, New Castle, Pa.*

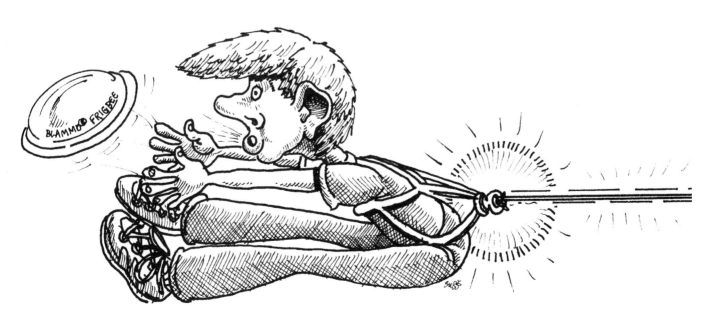

Ping-Pong Hula Doubles

Test your students' coordination and cooperation with a doubles Ping-Pong contest. Pair up a boy and a girl at each end of the table. Each player needs a paddle; each pair, a Hula Hoop.

The object of the game is to play a game of doubles Ping-Pong, though with teammates restrained within a single Hula Hoop. Pairs must move together during a volley, all the time keeping the Hula Hoop off the floor. Play short games—perhaps only to 11.

Invent whatever rules fit your situation and your kids. For instance, determine if pairs can use their free hand to keep the Hula Hoop up, or whether they must keep it up without hands—only by leaning opposite directions. *Michael Capps, East Flat Rock, N.C.*

Marshmallow Mouth to Mouth

Thread a marshmallow to the middle of a long, thin string of licorice. Put a player on each end of the licorice, then tell them this is an eating race (no hands allowed); first one to eat his or her way to the marshmallow—including the marshmallow—wins.

If this contact is too close for your comfort, center a pair of marshmallows four inches apart on the licorice. The first teen to reach and eat the closest marshmallow wins. *Rob Church, Glendale, Ariz.*

Popsicle Stick Frisbee

The more players, the better for this game—plus you'll need *lots* of Popsicle sticks (for just 20 players, you'll need a total of 240 sticks). Mark off a fairly large room or a gym similar to a soccer field (see illustration)—two halves separated by a center line, and a goal at each end (a goal should comprise about a quarter of a team's half of the floor).

Give every player a dozen Popsicle sticks, then

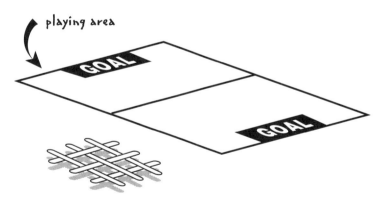

playing area

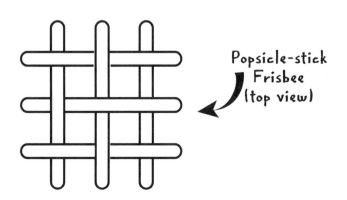

Popsicle-stick Frisbee (top view)

divide them into two teams. When the clock starts—

➤ **The offensive object** is for each player to quickly assemble a pair of Popsicle-stick Frisbees, then try to land as many as possible in their opponents' goal.

➤ **The defensive object** is to block Popsicle-stick Frisbees from entering their goal.

Rules:

➤ Players may block flying (or sliding) Popsicle-stick Frisbees any way they wish with their bodies.

➤ Broken sticks should be removed from the game.

➤ Players cannot cross the center line or enter their goals.

➤ Popsicle-stick Frisbees in the goals must stay; but Popsicle-stick Frisbees that land in the playing area may be used again.

➤ A team may want to designate some players offense, some defense, and some Frisbee builders—or all players can play all "positions."

The game continues for a predetermined duration of time, or until all Popsicle-stick Frisbees have landed in a goal. *Len Cuthbert, Hamilton, Ont., Canada*

Church Service Scavenger Hunt

Give copies of page 19 to your students just prior to a church service. (Choose a relatively informal service for this activity—one that doesn't require uninterrupted meditation, for example.) Compare answers in a following youth meeting. *Todd Wilson, Grand Rapids, Mich.*

Church Service Scavenger Hunt

Fill out this sheet during the service, then bring it with you to our meeting tonight.

1. The greeters:

2. Last one into the sanctuary:

3. One Bible person (other than Jesus) mentioned in today's Bible reading:

4. What the pastor is wearing:

5. The most encouraging answer to prayer you heard at church today:

6. Someone **really** into the service:

7. Someone **really** dressed up:

8. Someone in jeans:

9. Someone wearing green:

10. Number of children who went forward today for the children's message:

11. Length of sermon:

12. Largest family present:

13. Someone missing from church today:

14. The church season we're in now:

15. Number of youth group members in church:

CHAPTER THREE

CREATIVE COMMUNICATION

Priorities

Open the eyes of your kids to their values with this activity.

First, the preparation:

1. Make an envelope full of priorities for each student, like this: Look over the list of words on pages 21-22 and choose 10 or so that you think appeal most to your group's students. Photocopy the sheet (one copy per student), and from each sheet cut out the same 10 words—*plus the two slips that say "Jesus Christ" and "Life Itself."* Put each sheet's 12 slips into an envelope; when you're done, you should have as many envelopes as you'll have kids in the meeting.

2. Now make another set of envelopes: Cut out the verses at the bottom of each sheet along the dotted lines. (Depending on your youth group, the tone of the meeting, and your doctrinal views, you may or may not want to include the second verse on each slip. It's up to you.) Put each slip by itself in an unmarked, sealed envelope. But keep track of which slips are in which envelopes; there should be a subtle way for only you and a trusted volunteer to identify which Slip, A or B, is in each envelope. Give these two sets of envelopes to that volunteer to hold until later in the game.

3. Prepare a list of Bible trivia questions—from your previous Bible studies, from the game Bible Trivia, etc.

Now for the game:

Hand each student an envelope of priorities, a sheet of paper (to record answers to the trivia questions), and a pencil. Explain to them that in each envelope are a variety of things that are probably important to them. For each trivia question they answer incorrectly, they must forfeit one of their priorities out of their envelope—*except* the two priorities "Life Itself" and "Jesus Christ," which are fundamen-

tal to everything else.

Now ask the Bible trivia questions. After each question, students write their response, then you give the answer. Kids with correct answers do nothing; kids with incorrect answers forfeit one of their priority slips. Make the trivia questions difficult enough so that most kids are reduced to only two priority slips before long—"Life Itself" and "Jesus Christ."

Here's where your volunteer gets busy. Students who are trimmed down to only those two priorities, and then answer another trivial question incorrectly, have a choice to make: they sacrifice to your volunteer one or the other of their final two priorities. Your volunteer notes which one is handed to her—and gives the student one of her envelopes in exchange:

➤ A player who turns in the "Jesus Christ" priority (by implication valuing life itself above Jesus Christ) receives from the volunteer the sealed envelope containing slip A ("What good will it be for a man if he gains the whole world, yet forfeits his soul?").

➤ A player who turns in the priority "Life Itself" (by implication valuing Christ over physical life) gets a sealed envelope containing slip B ("Whoever finds his life will lose it, and whoever loses his life for my sake will find it").

Don't allow the students to open their envelopes until everyone has finished playing. Then separate the students into two or more groups according to which envelopes they received (or to grade in school, or to gender, etc.), and ask them to open their envelopes. This should lead to a great discussion on priorities.

For an extended game, include more than 12 priorities in the students' envelopes. *Michael Shipman, Chino, Calif.*

Priorities

LIFE ITSELF	AMERICAN RIGHTS
JESUS CHRIST	REPUTATION
MUSIC	TRAVEL
POPULARITY	WELL-FED
TELEPHONE	FAME
YOUR HOUSE	LEISURE
SPORTS	COMFORT
PARTIES	MONEY$$$
CAR	GOOD HEALTH
PARENTS	SUCCESS

Priorities (cont'd)

FAMILY	**YOUR NEIGHBORHOOD**
GIRL/BOYFRIEND	**PETS**
NEW CLOTHES	**YOUR PRIDE**
BEST FRIEND	**YOUR STEREO**
JOB	

SLIP A

What good will it be for a man if he gains the whole world, yet forfeits his soul? (Matthew 16:26)

Depart from me, you who are cursed, into the eternal fire prepared for the devil and his angels. (Matthew 25:41)

SLIP B

Whoever finds his life will lose it, and whoever loses his life for my sake will find it. (Matthew 10:39)

Welcome, you who are blessed by my Father; take your inheritance, the kingdom prepared for you since the creation of the world. (Matthew 25:34)

Lethal Labels

Labels can be wildly misleading. Here's a chance to teach kids to look inside for a true identity before judging someone quickly on appearances. This devotional offers a choice of two object lessons, a brief reading, and some relevant Scripture passages to explore with your students.

➤ **Object lesson 1.** Buy three kinds of dry breakfast cereal. One of them should be a kid's cereal—outlandish name, shapes, and colors (cereal color or box color). The other two should be the kind of cereal that, considering packaging and cereal name, just *look* and *sound* healthy—except that these two are actually *less* nutritious than the kid's cereal, according to the nutritional information on the sides of the boxes (especially fat content and calories per serving).

Show your group all three boxes and ask them to choose the healthiest cereal. (If a student asks you to read the nutritional information, just say you want to test their instinctive responses.) Discuss what makes a food healthy, making sure that *someone* mentions both fat content and calories.

Arrange the cereal boxes according to your students' judgment of least to most healthy. (They'll invariably rate the kid's cereal least healthy.) Now ask someone to read and compare the nutritional data—in particular, the fat content and calories—while you watch their jaws drop.

➤ **Object lesson 2.** Before your youth meeting remove the label from a can of soup, and carefully glue on a sauerkraut label. As you begin your devotional, hold up the can and ask, "Who here just *loves* sauerkraut?" After the groaning and gagging, ask them for one-word definitions of sauerkraut; you'll probably hear *gross, nauseating, sick, disgusting,* etc.

Then say something like, "How do you know this is sauerkraut? Do you always go by first impressions, or by how something appears on the surface?" Open the can as proof, explaining that we too easily label others solely because of how they look on the outside.

➤ **The reading.** Tell this story, or a similar one of your own:

On the first day of school, Jennifer saw a cute new boy. When she found out his name was Britt, she decided to try out the name when she saw him later in the hall.

"Hi, Britt," said Jennifer.

He didn't even turn around. At lunch she tried again—

and got ignored again. Jennifer got steamed. She vowed she'd never talk to him again. Not leaving it at that, all that afternoon she told her friends what a snob Britt was.

The next morning in the parking lot, she saw a woman she assumed was Britt's mom conversing with him—in sign language. She realized that Britt had never heard a word she said to him yesterday. And since he had never faced her and seen her lips, he didn't have a clue that she was talking to him.

➤ **Scripture passages.** Discuss Romans 14, verses 4 and 10-13. Notice the context—although this chapter's emphasis is making moral judgments about others, the passage also speaks about judging others falsely or prematurely.

Matthew 7:1 and 1 Samuel 16:7 speak clearly about examining the contents carefully if you want to know the truth.

There is possible parental application here, too. Parents may reevaluate their estimation of some teenagers if they become conscious of how they label kids as rebellious, untrustworthy, or lazy. They may recognize that kids frequently live down to those expectations. *Steve Fortosis, Portland, Ore.; and Mike McKay, Los Gatos, Calif.*

Rotating Sunday School

Liven up Sunday school for junior high kids with short attention spans by keeping them on the move.

Brainstorm with your staff of teachers possible content and illustrations for an upcoming Sunday school lesson. Ask each teacher to take one of the ideas the group comes up with and prepare a mini-lesson for the designated Sunday. Length? Probably five to 10 minutes, depending on how many mini-lessons you'll offer and how long your entire class time lasts. You may want to allow time for a closing all-group session.

As students arrive that Sunday, randomly assign them to where teachers are waiting. Signal the end of each mini-lesson with a gong or other jarring instrument, signal the end of the first lesson and explain to the kids how to find their next class—for example, rotate clockwise to the next teacher or room. By the end of Sunday school, all the junior highers should have met with all the teachers. *Jeff Elliott, Cleveland, Tenn.*

Hit Personalities

Their favorite songs can reflect teenagers' personalities and interests. So ask them to bring you the album containing their favorite song—but in a bag, to keep it secret from the others.

Either at that meeting or a later one, play at least part of each song, and let the group guess whose

favorite it is. Then let that student (or students, since more than one may select the same song) explain how the song reflects his or her personality.

There's even display potential here: write the song titles and the choosers' names on poster-board "CDs" to display on the walls. Sherry Wingert, Oakland, Neb.

Homeless Scavenger Hunt

Expose your youth group to the plight of the homeless with this unusual spin on a pizza feed and scavenger hunt. It results in a surprise overnighter—outside—so parents should be made aware of this beforehand (and then sworn to secrecy). Don't do this activity if the weather is severe.

Offer no details about the party but the date, starting time, and place. Begin the evening with a normal youth party. Play games, eat, and have fun. After an hour or two, begin the scavenger hunt. Send the teams out to find items *that can be donated to the homeless*. Assign point values: 10 points for a sleeping

bag, 5 points for a blanket, 10 for a jacket, 5 for a big cardboard box, 20 for a tent, etc. When the teams have completed their hunt and returned to the church, tally the points and award the winning team with a prize.

This is where you describe what you really have in mind for the evening: a homeless experience. Explain that you are having an all-night lock-*out* and that the only things they can use are the items they just collected. The winning team gets to pick their blankets, jackets, boxes, and other supplies first. Then lock the doors and watch the kids adapt.

In the morning discuss what the group learned (usually a new appreciation for home!), then take the collected material to a donation center for the homeless. *Tim Brown, Riddle, Ore.*

B.I.G.

Warm up your group by asking a couple kids to tell their biggest moment in life. Then read some stats from *The Guinness Book of Records* that you selected earlier—the biggest man, the biggest pizza on record, the biggest mushroom.

Have someone read Ephesians 5:1. Then ask your group what *big* has to do with that verse. Did they catch it? Read the verse again. God's greatest desire is for his people to *Be Imitators of God*—B.I.G. people. In small groups, students can take turns recalling how they've seen someone else imitate God. On what occasions have they themselves come close to imitating God?

End with a prayer commissioning your students to be B.I.G. people. For more study, try Ephesians 5:1-17, which challenges Christians to take three B.I.G. steps in order to be B.I.G. people for God:
1. Walk in love (vv. 1-7)
2. Walk in light (vv. 8-14)
3. Walk in wisdom (vv. 15-17)

Tommy Baker, Florence, Ky.

Scatter Worship

Does your youth group sit together during worship each Sunday? Get the pastor's approval, then schedule a Scatter Worship for a particular Sunday.

Explain to the youths what a Scatter Worship

looks like. Before the service begins, or during a fellowship hymn, or at another appropriate time in the worship service, the teenagers scatter (inconspicuously) throughout the sanctuary. In groups no larger than two or three, they must sit with the elderly, visitors, single parents, or anyone who looks lonely or who they know needs a word of encouragement. Teens can offer friendship and encouragement to other church members while joining in worship with them. *John Peters, Cleveland, Tenn.*

CHAPTER FOUR

YOUTH GROUP LEADERSHIP

Stress-Week Baskets

Shortly before final exams begin, get together with other youth workers to assemble survival baskets for all your senior highers.

Easter baskets, fake grass, and cellophane can be purchased very inexpensively right after Easter. Remove the handles from the baskets (this makes them look less like Easter baskets) and line them with fake grass.

Then fill the baskets with granola bars, nuts, M & Ms, fruit, high-caffeine soda pop, pretzels, Life Savers, gum—whatever your kids enjoy. Cover the baskets with cellophane and tie them with curly ribbon in their school colors. Add a humorous card with a note like "We're all praying for you during this stressful time."

Deliver the baskets during the Sunday meeting before finals week, or make home deliveries early in the week. The baskets give tangible evidence that you know some of the difficulties your students are facing. *Sally West, Tucson, Ariz.*

Golden Hit Awards

Recognize the positive traits in your teens with "Golden Hit Awards." Collect some old 45 or 33 1/3 vinyl records—ones you don't have to return. Heat them in a 200-degree oven for five to seven minutes, then shape them into "trophy bowls" with ruffled edges. (Use oven mitts to handle the hot discs.) Let the records cool on foil, then spray them with gold spray paint.

Create a variety of awards—for a bubbly person-ality, great smile, wonderful friend, good listener, etc. *Sherry Wingert, Oakland, Neb.*

Know Your Vowels Card

Commitments from school, sports, and family can pressure students to back away from church youth group. A Know Your Vowels card is a mild reminder of small things they can do to help themselves, the group, and you.

Attend	as many things as you can.
Encourage	your friends—avoid put-downs and gossip.
Invite	your friends—they won't come if you don't ask them.
Oppose	Satan by praying for the group, the church, and the leaders.
Use	your spiritual gifts—God gave them to you for a reason.

Photocopy this sample (or write your own) on card stock of a vibrant color. Mail them to kids or hand them out at events. Kids can put them in their bedroom mirror, on their wall, inside their school locker door, taped to their car dashboard, etc. Encourage them to pray for the group each time they see the card—and to do what the card recommends. *Brett C. Wilson, Terre Haute, Ind.*

School Logos

Even if you're artistically challenged, you can decorate your youth room with large, colorful reproductions of the logos for each school represented by members of your youth group. The completed project is an exercise of unity in diversity—plus it breaks down school rivalries.

Get copies of the logos from each of the schools; better yet, a local screen printer may already have logos from all the schools in your area. Make a transparency of each logo and project it to the size you want on a sheet of poster board. Trace the image in pencil, outline it with black permanent marker, add the appropriate colors, and cut it out. The result is a professional-looking logo ready to mount on your wall. And be sure to recruit your teenagers to help. *Tom Lytle, Marion, Ohio*

Radio Dramas

With a microphone, a couple of tape decks, and a little creativity, youth groups can produce fascinating radio programs (whether or not they're ever actually broadcast on the radio) that incorporate adventure, comedy, and drama. After all, once upon a time this was the ultimate family entertainment.

Radio dramas can be perfect for teens who normally shy away from being on stage—but just may excel behind a microphone. Goofs are corrected easily, and copies of the finished tape can be given to each participant. Almost any script can be adapted for radio drama. Teens can be creative and make up material that fits their own group.

Programs can take the form of an interview or a drama. For an interview, give the questions to the interview subject before the interview, so the subject can think through his or her responses before the actual recording.

Drama takes a bit more preparation—but it's a lot of fun, too. Here are some guidelines for building a drama script:

➤ Set a time limit for each of the brainstorming sessions and decisions that follow—say five to 10 minutes.

➤ Establish the personalities of two to four characters—give them names, occupations, etc. Then give them a general setting—school, the moon, Calcutta, etc.

➤ Identify the key issues your characters will face. (This will determine the theme and the purpose of the drama.)

➤ Consider how these issues might be portrayed and resolved in a drama. Use flow charts so that everyone can see how the story line or lines will be drawn. Break the story into scenes. Think visually, even though this is a radio drama, since listeners will visualize in their minds what they're hearing.

➤ Now break into groups and assign each group one scene to write. Remember the time considerations, and determine how much time each scene will be allotted. Make sure the transitions between the scenes are smooth.

➤ Determine what action you will describe or convey with the use of a sound-effects tape. Select music and a few key sound effects.

➤ When the drama is written, check that the message you decided to convey is clear to the listener.

➤ Rehearse and time the scenes, incorporating the sound effects and music.

➤ Edit the scenes as necessary.

➤ Record.

Bill Swedberg, Renton, Wash.

CHAPTER FIVE

SPECIAL EVENTS

Money Hunt and Auction

Invite kids to an old-fashioned auction where the bidding is done with play money. Ask them to bring the items to be auctioned—old appliances that still work, fishing poles, not-quite-antique dishes or jewelry boxes. The items should have some appeal to potential bidders.

Before the activity begins, hide envelopes containing play money and write out clues to help the kids find the money. The search can cover territory as broad as the neighborhood (using cars the teams search telephone booths, grocery stores, various landmarks, etc.), or as confined as your church grounds.

Start the event by forming teams and handing out the clues to each team. Give a time limit for the treasure hunt, at which time the kids meet back at the starting point for the auction. When they return, teams divide the money found among the team members. Then start the bidding. *Mike Kwok, Mooresville, N.C.*

tude so they understand that they are appreciated.

From there, send them to a location where they will find flowers...then to a restaurant where the youth group has already paid for an elegant meal...and maybe end up at a theater, bowling alley, concert, etc. (for which tickets have already been purchased). Choose activities that each honoree especially enjoys. *Cheryl Ehlers, East Point, Ga.*

Thanks, Pastor

Give a progressive gift to say thanks to your pastors or youth workers. Send them a letter asking them to reserve a certain evening for this activity—but give no details of what you have planned. If they need it, offer free baby-sitting for their children. Tell them only when and where to go on the given night. Only after they arrive will they learn what's next.

For example, you could ask them to meet at the church, where all the young people are gathered to roast their pastor with soft drinks in champagne glasses. Have fun, but also be serious in your grati-

Vehicular Sardines

This game is an adaptation of the game, "Sardines," in which two people hide, and everyone who finds them must hide with them until eventually everyone has found them. "Vehicular Sardines" adds the fun of a hunt on wheels to the original game.

Divide your students into groups of four or five, depending on the size and type of vehicles available.

Assign one adult to each group to ensure safety. Select one group and send them to a destination you have chosen (an accessible one, such as a park, tennis court, mall, etc.). Give the hiding car about 10 or 15 minutes lead, and give them these reminders:

➤ They must get out of their vehicle when they reach the destination.

➤ They must leave the vehicle in plain view at the destination. (The car is a legitimate clue for seeking teams.)

➤ They must hide together, not as individuals, and may not change hiding places after once hidden.

When the hiding group has left, hand out to all the seeking groups a map with cryptic clues to the destination. Set a time—45 minutes or an hour—by which they should return to the church whether or not they've found the hiding group.

For even more fun, send a camcorder along with the hiding group to videotape the other groups finding them—and squishing together, trying to make room for each other. Finish the evening back at church with food and a premier showing of the video. (For a shorter, on-site "Sardine" game, see "Wireless Sardines" on page 13.) *Paul Coleman, Longview, Tex.*

Where's Waldo?

Rumor has it he may *still* be lingering in a mall near you. So don't look in a book—take your group to the mall to look for a real, live Waldo.

To play this version of "Where's Waldo?" have a youth worker or parent dress like Waldo, or at least wear something—a tie, stocking cap, conspicuous socks, etc.—that bears the trademark red-and-white Waldo look. In addition to Waldo himself, plant 10 Carriers of Waldo's Possessions in the mall, too, each one carrying or wearing one these:

➤ Scroll   ➤ Message in a bottle
➤ Flag   ➤ Skates
➤ A deck of cards   ➤ Bird's nest
➤ Baseball bat   ➤ Football player
➤ Duck   ➤ A cane

With your volunteers planted at the mall, and after the kids have arrived at church, explain the game. Divide into teams of three or four, and give each team a copy of the sheet on page 31. Before you release them to the mall (or other area you've chosen), give them a

Waldoesque pep talk—something like this:

> *Continue on your journey and never rest until you have found Waldo and all his possessions. For in finding them, you will help Waldo understand the purpose of his journey—and then he will perceive the truth about himself. Let the search begin!*

Kids should meet back at the church (or a designated location) as soon as they find Waldo and all of his items, or when the time expires, whichever comes first. *Tommy Baker, Florence, Ky.*

Youth Versus Experience

In this parent-student event, kids compete against parents in everything from volleyball, softball, and basketball, to relays and food-eating contests. This can be an annual event, with a rotating trophy for the winning team each year. A wall plaque can display the names of past winners.

After the games, host a barbecue or potluck that lets parents get acquainted with the youth workers. This activity is particularly useful if parents don't regularly attend the church. *Brian Krum, Reedley, Calif.*

Progressive Superbowl Party

Or celebrate *any* major sporting event with this party plan.

Divide the evening according to periods, quarters, or innings (depending on what sport you're watching). Then enlist different parents to host portions of the evening in their homes. For a Progressive Superbowl Party, for instance, you could use as few as two homes (pregame and first half, and half-time and second half) or as many as six (pregame, first quarter, second quarter, half-time, third quarter, fourth quarter).

Ask each host to supply snacks that fit the event (cookies shaped like footballs, ballpark hot dogs, etc.). Teens may wear the colors of the team they are rooting for. When choosing the different homes, take location into consideration so that you won't miss much of the game during travel from place to place. *Tim Gross, Lincoln, Neb.*

Where's Waldo?

ITEM	VERIFYING SIGNATURE	POINTS
1. Waldo's scroll	_____	7,000 points
2. Waldo's message in a bottle	_____	8,000 points
3. Waldo's flag	_____	2,000 points
4. Waldo's skates	_____	3,000 points
5. Waldo's deck of cards	_____	6,000 points
6. Waldo's duck	_____	4,000 points
7. Waldo's bird nest	_____	2,000 points
8. Waldo's baseball bat	_____	2,000 points
9. Waldo's football player	_____	5,000 points
10. Waldo's cane	_____	8,000 points
11. Waldo himself	_____	1,000 points

RULES OF THE GAME

1. Be kind, courteous, and polite at all times. Avoid being rude and obnoxious.

2. When approaching someone ask, "Are you Waldo?" or "Is that Waldo's —?"

3. The first team to find Waldo and all of his items and get to the designated location—
   or the team with the most points—is the winner.

4. We will meet at _____ at _____.
                    PLACE   TIME

5. When you find Waldo or his belongings, ask the person you found to sign your game sheet
   for verification.

**So onward, ever upward, O noble friends of Waldo! Join your
hero on his fantastic journey. Let the Great Waldo Search begin!**

Video Hit Squad

This camcorder scavenger hunt can be played by any number of groups. Each group needs a camcorder (with a fresh battery and a blank tape), 20 quarters ($5), and an adult chaperon to drive each carload of teenagers to various locations (and to ensure fair play).

Use the list on page 34, or create a similar one of your own. *Students should not see this list.* (A note about the hits on this list: if you compile your own, separate those that could be easily recorded back to back, at the same location—like a sign that displays the time and a sign that displays the temperature.) Make as many copies as there will be teams ("mobs"), and give them to the "Godfather," who sits by the phone at home base.

On the day of the event, divide your kids into mobs and let them choose a mob name. Each mob designates a Hit Man who operates the camcorder and a Liaison who calls the Godfather from the various phone booths. (Or mob members can rotate these duties among themselves.) Explain that the Godfather has 10 targets (or however many you've chosen) for them to "hit" with their camcorder—but he will reveal those targets only one at a time. For their first target, they can drive to any pay phone (if you want, stipulate how far they must drive before using a pay phone).

Guidelines that each mob should follow:

➤ No speeding. Obey all traffic laws.
➤ All members of a mob must stay together at all times.
➤ Be sure you know your home-base phone number.
➤ No one in your mob may appear in your own video.
➤ Make all Godfather calls from a pay phone, using only the quarters that were issued to you.
➤ Return to the church at the designated time, whether or not you've hit all the possible targets.

Then let them go. In their first call the Godfather asks them what number hit they want first (1-17). The mob chooses, then the Godfather tells them what that hit is (plus any bonus). After they hang up, the mob hits its target, calls the Godfather to report a successful hit, then gets its next target. A typical exchange might go like this:

Mob's Liaison: Godfather? This is the "Capone" mob. We're at Joe's Pizza Palace on the corner of Main Street and Davis Drive. We just hit number five—a vehicle filling up with gas. We got the bonus, too—it was a motorcycle.
Godfather: *(jotting down on the score-sheet the time of call, the location the mob is calling from, and the points the mob earned)* Nice job, Capone. Your next target is someone washing a car, for 500 points.
Mob's Liaison: Got it. 'Bye.

Because of the time limit you've given them, the mobs will quickly figure out that the bonuses may or may not be worth the minutes they eat up waiting for (or setting up!) the bonus scenarios. Should they use their time quickly hitting a dozen targets at 500 points each, or should they hit only six or seven targets—but accumulate some 1,000-point bonuses along the way?

Mobs return to church when they've hit all 10 targets or, at any rate, by the deadline (even if they haven't hit all 10). Record each mob's arrival time back at the base (an earlier arrival time might break a tie in point scores). To the mobs that return to church before the deadline, having hit all 10 targets, award a bonus of 2,000 points. Penalize mobs 500 points for each minute over the deadline they're tardy. Have the Godfather on hand to tally the points and determine which mob rules the city.

After the big mob fight, serve candy kisses so that mobs can kiss and make up—while the entire group views the videos to confirm each mob's claims. (You may want an objective judge on hand to settle disputes.) *Brett Wilson, Terre Haute, Ind.*

Stuffed Animal Night

Return your teenagers to their childhood, if only for an evening. Get the word out for them to bring their favorite stuffed animals to a youth group meeting. Pile the menagerie in the middle of the room and play games that help your group think about being kids again.

Adapt games so they have a teddy bear/stuffed-animal flavor:

➤ Do the over-under basketball relay with a teddy bear.

➤ Indoor "Nerfketball" (*Ideas 17*) becomes "Stuffed Animal Dunk."

➤ Play "Longjohn Stuff" (*Ideas 1*), only stuff the longjohns with stuffed animals instead of balloons—and the kids wearing the longjohns must also wear Care Bear masks.

➤ Some of the "kiddie" games in the "Blast from the Past" party in *Junior High Game Nights* (Youth Specialties) work well.

Then tone down the evening by circling up and letting kids spend some time sharing explaining what makes their stuffed animals so special. You might focus on unconditional love, for instance (both stuffed animals and God love no matter what). Finish the evening with a "story time": hand out Graham crackers, then read *The Velveteen Rabbit* while kids sit with their stuffed animals. (For a stuffed-animal activity suitable for fifth and sixth graders at camp, see page 49.) *Mark Jackson, Nashville, Tenn.*

VIDEO HIT SQUAD
Godfather's Hit List and Scoresheet for _____ Mob
MOB NAME

Hit (with point value)	Score	Time of call (following this hit)	Calling from— (location)
1. Someone buying a paper (500) Bonus: the paper is a *USA Today* (1,000)			
2. A couple walking holding hands or arms around each other (500) Bonus: they kiss (1,000)			
3. A taxi cab (500) Bonus: there's an illuminated light on top (1,000) Double bonus: a passenger is getting in or out of the cab (1,000)			
4. A sign that displays the current time (500)			
5. Someone filling up their vehicle with gasoline (500) Bonus: it's a truck or a motorcycle (1,000)			
6. Someone washing an automobile (500)			
7. A transaction at a drive-thru (500) Bonus: the transaction is *not* food related (1,000)			
8. Someone with a two-liter soft drink (500) Bonus: the drink is orange flavored (1,000)			
9. Someone using an automatic teller machine (500) Bonus: it's a walk-up ATM (1,000) Double bonus: it's a drive-up ATM, and the vehicle is a van (1,000) Triple bonus: the van drives *backwards* through the ATM (1,000)			
10. Someone eating pizza (500) Bonus: the eater is eating standing up (1,000)			
11. Someone washing their windshield (500) Bonus: at a gas station (1,000) Double bonus: the gas station attendant is washing the window (1,000)			
12. A sign that displays the current temperature (500) Bonus: the sign displays in degrees Celsius (1,000)			
13. A sign containing a person's name (500) Bonus: the name is a biblical name (1,000)			
14. Someone buying a can of soda from a vending machine (500) Bonus: the person buys two cans (1,000) Double bonus: the two cans are both Diet Cokes (1,000)			
15. A railroad car (500) Bonus: the railroad car is moving (1,000) Double bonus: the engine pulling the railroad car sounds its horn (1,000)			
16. Someone using the telephone (500) Bonus: the person is in a phone booth (1,000)			
17. An American flag hung on a flag pole (500) Bonus: the flag is extended by the wind (1,000)			

	Score		
TOTAL			
ARRIVAL BONUS			
ARRIVAL PENALTY			
GRAND TOTAL			

CHAPTER SIX

SKETCHES, SKITS, AND DRAMAS

Match of the Generations

Perform this sketch that begins on page 36 for an event attended by both teenagers and their parents, whether a Youth Sunday service or a fundraising banquet. The dialogue strikes a familiar chord among family members and easily provokes later discussions in your meetings or between parents and their children. *Luis Cataldo and Bill Moucka, Hudson, Ohio*

A Lake Excursion

In this highly participatory skit on page 38, the characters (and human "props") simply act out what the narrator reads—no rehearsals necessary! It's based on Mark 4:35-41, which describes the Galilee sailing jaunt during which Jesus slept through a storm. This skit makes an effective springboard for a study of the Mark passage, or for topical discussions about adolescent pressures and stress. *Molly Halter, Poland, Ohio*

Bungee Jumping with God

On page 39 is a simple sketch for two characters that explores the risks of faith in terms of bungee jumping. *Steve Wunderink, Allendale, Mich.*

Take Up Your Cross

This six-scene drama can comprise an entire evening's program. Allow enough preparation time to memorize lines, rehearse, and make the props. It begins on page 40. *James L. Wing, Niles, Mich.*

MATCH OF THE GENERATIONS

Characters

Mom (cast an adult in this role)
Dad (adult)
The Kid (student)
Big Sister (student)
Ring announcer and referee

Props

4 standards joined by 3 cords (like those in banks to mark lines; banquet facilities usually have these available)
2 chairs
1 loud bell
2 sets of boxing gloves

The cords and standards are unused at the moment, off to the side. Two chairs, facing the audience, are center stage. **Dad** *is reading the paper, seated in one chair, feet propped up on the other.* **The Kid** *enters.*

KID: Dad, I'm outta here.
DAD: Where are you going, Kid?
KID: Just out.
DAD: Well, where's out?
KID: I don't know, just around.
DAD: This is not going to be another one of those, is it?
KID: Looks like it, Dad.

(As the **Announcer** *is speaking, the cast uses the standards and cords to make a three-sided boxing ring. The chairs are moved to the two upstage corners of the ring;* **Dad** *and* **The Kid** *take their places there. Beside The Kid stands* **Big Sister**; *beside Dad stands* **Mom**. *The four of them are busy putting gloves on* **Dad** *and* **The Kid***)*

ANNOUNCER: Ladies and gentlemen! Tonight's main event...the challenge match of the generations. *(pointing as he speaks)* In this corner, weighing in at one spare tire over his ideal weight, overworked and underappreciated: Dad. And in this corner, equipped with driver's license, girlfriend, and all the right answers: The Kid. In Dad's corner will be his lifelong companion, Mom. And in The Kid's corner will be the former champion, Big Sister. The rules are... One: no cheap shots. Two: Dad, no calling Mom into the ring for help. Three: Kid, no comparing yourself to your sister. Now go to your corners and when you hear the bell, come out fighting.
(Bell rings. Gloves on, **Dad** *and* **The Kid** *move to the center of the ring, circling each other, gloves up, taking occasional, tentative jabs at each other)*
DAD: Where are you going?
KID: Out.
DAD: Where?
KID: Out.
DAD: Where?
KID: Out.
ANNOUNCER: Okay, break.
DAD: What are you going to be doing?
KID: Nothing.
DAD: Nothing is the kind of activity that ends up in the police blotter.
KID: Dad, you know there's nothing to do in this town. We'll probably get a pizza and rent a movie.
DAD: What movie will you be renting?
KID: I don't know. We'll just find one.
DAD: I just don't want you watching any garbage.
KID: Okay. We'll probably get "The Little Mermaid."
DAD: Who will you be with?
KID: You know, John, Joe, Jack.
DAD: John who? Joe who? Jack who? Do I know these guys?
KID: Yeah, Dad. You met them when you made me do Cub Scouts.
DAD: Well, how can I remember that long ago? Have I met their parents?

KID: They were at the last football game. I think you saw them there.

DAD: I don't remember. Well, whose house are you going to?

KID: Probably Joe's house.

DAD: Are his parents going to be home?

KID: I don't know.

DAD: You know, we finished the game room so we could have people over. Why don't you all come here?

KID: Because you guys are always here.

DAD: Well, what did your mother say about all this?

KID: She said it was okay with her if it was okay with you.

*(Bell rings. **Dad** and **The Kid** go to their respective corners)*

MOM: (to **Dad**) Remember to ask more questions. When will he be home? Has he done his homework? What about cleaning up his room? Just keep asking questions, and try to be fair.

SISTER: (to **The Kid**) You did a great job. You really danced around those questions. Just remember, be vague. When he asks about what time you'll be home, he'll probably insist on getting specific, so shoot for one o'clock and settle for midnight. Just try to get out the door as soon as possible.

*(Bell rings; **Dad** and **The Kid** return to the ring as before)*

KID: Dad, I gotta go.

DAD: Just a minute. I have some more questions. When will you be home?

KID: When the movie's over. Probably late.

DAD: When's late?

KID: I don't know. Maybe one o'clock.

DAD: One o'clock! That's too late. You be home by 10:30.

KID: 10:30! None of my friends have to be home by 10:30.

DAD: Well, if all your friends drove off a cliff, would you follow them?

KID: *(rolling his eyes)* Not <u>that</u> one again.

DAD: I want to be fair. Let's see. How about eleven?

KID: But I have to take Tracy home. And she doesn't have to be home until 11:45.

DAD: Okay, you can be home at 11:45, too.

KID: But I have to drive her home and then get home after that.

DAD: Okay, let's compromise. How about...you be home by midnight.

KID: Okay, Dad.

DAD: Now. Is your homework done?

KID: Dad, it's Friday night.

DAD: There's no law against studying on a Friday. Mark next door studies on Friday night.

KID: Mark's a geek.

DAD: But Mark got accepted at Harvard.

KID: I'll get in somewhere, Dad.

DAD: Well, is your room clean?

KID: I'll clean it tomorrow. I'll have all day to work on it.

*(Bell rings. **Dad** and **The Kid** go to their corners)*

SISTER: *(To **The Kid**)* Remember to get money for gas before you leave—and whatever you do, don't get into a discussion about getting a job.

DAD: *(To **Mom**)* Why do we always argue like this?

MOM: *(To **Dad**)* I think it's that we see so much potential in him, and we want the best for him. By the way, I just gave him $20 this morning, so he shouldn't need any money.

*(Bell rings and **Dad** and **The Kid** enter the ring once again)*

KID: Gotta go, Dad. Oh, and I need $20.

DAD: Your mother just gave you $20.

KID: I had to eat.

DAD: Why can't you ever eat at home? We have plen—

KID: *(interrupting)* But the car needs gas, so I really need some money.

DAD: Why can't you use your allowance for gas?

KID: It's all gone.

DAD: Where did it go?

KID: I had to eat.

DAD: If you had a job, you wouldn't have to be asking for money all the time. I noticed a "Help Wanted" sign at the ice cream store just last—

KID: *(interrupting)* Gotta go, Dad. My friends are waiting. Be back by one o'clock. *(exits past **Big Sister**—and gives her a thumbs-up signal on his way out)*

DAD: Be home by midnight!

END

A Lake Excursion
An extemporaneous skit

Characters and "Props"
Narrator • Disciples (12 people) • Jesus
Boat (8-12 people) • Sail • Cushion • Wind (4-5 people) • Waves (4-5 people)

Jesus and his disciples had spent a long day of teaching and preaching by the lake and evening had come. Jesus said to the disciples, "Let's go over to the other side of the lake and find a McDonald's." With great enthusiasm, everyone said, "Yeah!" and rapidly nodded their heads up and down. They were all so dog-tired they were hanging onto each other in order to stand up. They all climbed into the boat.

Jesus was tired too, of course. He climbed in the boat, walked directly to the back, lay his head down on the cushion, and immediately began snoring.

The tiny fishing boat set out from shore, rocking gently in the quiet waters of Lake Galilee. While Jesus snored, the disciples leaned against the sides of the boat, laughing and talking. The wind swayed softly over the lake, and the boat's sail gently followed the direction of the little breezes. The waves sweetly lapped the sides of the boat.

And everyone was thinking of a Big Mac, fries, and a chocolate shake, to go.

But out of nowhere came a furious squall. *(At this point the narrator asks the audience to stomp their feet and clap their hands to provide sound effects for the storm)* The waves broke over the sides of the boat. The sail swung around and around on the mast, bonking the disciples on their heads. The wind and the waves rocked the boat madly—its occupants were pitched first to one side of the boat, and then to the other. And still the sail swung around, bonking more disciples. The boat continued heaving—and soon the disciples were, too, leaning over the sides of the boat. It got gross.

Finally in desperation, one of the disciples recovered enough to grab the sail and hang on to it, to keep it from swinging around and bonking more people on the head. Though he was still seasick, he hung onto that sail. The poor sail was a mess.

But in the back of the boat, the pitching boat only put Jesus into a deeper sleep—and produced louder snores. The cushion rocked too, of course, but it didn't snore.

The disciples wildly scrambled around and over each another in desperation. Some began bailing. Others shouted to each other questions like "Where's Jesus?" "Can't he help us?" "What's he doing?"

So on their hands and knees, they all crawled to the back of the boat and surrounded Jesus, who was still sleeping peacefully, snoring, rocking gently, his head on the cushion.

Together, the disciples shouted to Jesus, "Teacher! Don't you care if we drown?" They shouted it again, in unison this time, because they didn't do it too well the first time.

Finally, Jesus rolled over, sat up on top of the cushion, yawned, and rubbed his eyes. "Hey, what's up?" he asked sleepily.

It only took him a moment to grasp the desperate situation, so he got up and walked to the middle of the boat. Here he could view everything—the stressed-out disciples, the rocking boat, the sail still thrashing about, the crashing waves, the violent wind. He stretched out his arms and cried out in a loud voice, "Waves! Be still!"

Immediately, the waves fell flat on their faces outside the boat and lay still, as good waves should do. Then Jesus cried out again, "Wind! Die down!"

Immediately the wind died down all over on top of the waves and lay still on top of the waves like good wind should do.

The boat stopped rocking, the sail stopped spinning about, and everything was calm, quiet, and just plain cool. Jesus looked over everything, looked at the wind, the waves, the boat, the sail, the cushion—even the disciples. He looked at the disciples a long time. He looked first at one, then at another—at all of them, one at a time.

Finally he said softly, "Why are you so afraid? Do you still have no faith?"

The disciples, still terrified and huddled together, said to each other, "Who is this man? Even the wind and waves obey him!"

But then the disciples all breathed a huge, loud sigh of relief. A very huge, loud sigh. Then they jumped up and hugged Jesus and thanked him. All at once. Big group hug. And the little fishing boat sailed calmly to the other side of the lake, sail flapping happily in the wind.

When they landed, the disciples climbed out of the boat, safe and sound, and decided to go, not to McDonald's after all, but to Subway instead.

END

Bungee Jumping with God

A Sketch for Two Actors

CHARACTERS:

INSTRUCTOR, JUMPER

*On a bridge or in a bucket on a crane, a novice is working up nerve to make his or her first bungee jump. To the audience's perception, the rope is anchored somewhere above the two characters, so the rope should hang down from above and be tied to the **Jumper's** ankles, the slack coiled at his feet.*

JUMPER: *(peering nervously over the edge)* Sure this is safe?

INSTRUCTOR: Of course it is. Hundreds of people have already done it.

JUMPER: Yeah, but what kind of shape are they in now?

INSTRUCTOR: It all depends on how you jump.

JUMPER: Wha—what do you mean?

INSTRUCTOR: Well, there are several ways you can do this. Some are safer than others. Some are just plain stupid.

JUMPER: Stupid?

INSTRUCTOR: Some people jump without being tied to anything solid. They insist on tying their own cord—won't trust anyone else to tie it for them—and, of course, the knot usually comes loose when the jumper puts any stress on it.

JUMPER: That is stupid.

INSTRUCTOR: What's even dumber is leaping without being tied to anything at all—which is what some people actually do. They just jump, and on their way down look up at me with that "See? I can do anything!" look. "It's easy!" they yell to those climbing up, as they fall past them.

JUMPER: What happens to them?

INSTRUCTOR: I've never seen one come back up for a second jump.

JUMPER: *(swallowing hard)* Oh...

INSTRUCTOR: Don't worry. As long as you jump the right way, nothing will happen to you. Lots of people jump regularly—every day of their lives, in fact.

JUMPER: Every day?

INSTRUCTOR: Sure. Once you do it the right way, it gets more familiar the next time, and then you go higher and take bigger jumps. That's how you build the faith up.

JUMPER: *(looking down, still nervous)* By jumping?

INSTRUCTOR: Sure. The first time is always the hardest. After that leap of faith, it's easier because you know it's safe—when done the right way, of course.

JUMPER: So I can't tie this thing myself?

INSTRUCTOR: Nope, not if you want to be safe.

JUMPER: So what do I do? Thanks to the fog, I can't see the bottom and *(looking up, squinting)* I can't see through the mist what this is tied to up there.

INSTRUCTOR: That's the adventure of being who you are.

JUMPER: Who I am?

INSTRUCTOR: You're a Christian, right?

JUMPER: Well...yes.

INSTRUCTOR: There's the adventure. Since you can't see the bottom—

JUMPER: *(panicky)* There is a bottom down there, isn't there?

INSTRUCTOR: Sure, but it's not the same for everybody. What's under that fog is different for everyone.

JUMPER: Well, what is it for me?

INSTRUCTOR: *(shrugs)* Dunno.

JUMPER: *(giving the cord a couple tugs)* Okay, so what's the top end of the bungee cord tied to?

INSTRUCTOR: Up in that mist, if you do it right, Jesus is holding the cord.

JUMPER: He is? *(looking up, straining to see)* Really? I can't see him.

INSTRUCTOR: Neither can I. But rest assured he's up there. If you saw him holding, would that help?

JUMPER: It sure would!

INSTRUCTOR: But he told you, over and over, that he would be there holding that cord for you whenever you ask him to.

JUMPER: Yeah, but—

INSTRUCTOR: And he's provided you the stories of many successful jumpers—Abraham, for example. Man, could he jump. And Moses and Daniel and Esther and Mary and Paul...

JUMPER: Yeah, but—

INSTRUCTOR: So why on earth do you need to see him up there?

JUMPER: *(tentatively)* I guess I don't, as long as I know he's there...

INSTRUCTOR: He's there all right. All you have to do is ask him to hold the cord while you jump, and he'll do it. He promises.

JUMPER: What about this end of the cord? *(looking down at his ankles)* Will he tie it good and tight on my feet, too?

INSTRUCTOR: That's our job. Why don't we tighten 'em up before you jump? I'll show you how to do it. *(kneels, begins to explain to **Jumper** how to tighten the cords, etc.)*

END

TAKE UP YOUR CROSS

Characters:

Narrator
Sammy Slick
Matt
Megan

Carla
Simon
Tom
Jenny

NARRATOR: *It's fairly easy to be a Christian—at least, it's easy to <u>say</u> you're a Christian when it's convenient. Christians don't have signs around their necks that announce their faith. But think about Christ's words in Mark 8:34: "If anyone would come after me, he must deny himself and take up his cross and follow me." What if Christians were <u>required</u> to carry crosses as mandatory symbols of their faith?*

SCENE 1

*Inside Crosses Galore, a mall shop that sells all varieties of crosses. Behind the counter is a salesman. **Carla**, a new Christian, enters the shop.*

SAMMY SLICK: Hel-lo. Come in, come in. How can I help you?

CARLA: *(with enthusiasm)* I just accepted Christ as my Savior, and I'd like to get a cross.

SLICK: Well, you've come to the right place. My name is Sammy Slick, but you can call me S.S. *(making a hissing, snake-like sound)*. I'm your friend—and I know just what you need.

CARLA: Great!

SLICK: *(taking out a gold cross about a foot tall)* We happen to be in the middle of a 24-hour sale, and for only $24.95 you can go home wearing this beautiful 24-carat gold filigree cross. We'll even throw in the chain.

CARLA: *(hesitating)* Oh...well, this isn't quite what I was looking for...

SLICK: I understand. It's too <u>big</u>. I know exactly how you feel. *(pulls out a tiny cross)* Listen, here's a little sweetheart that I can let go for $19.95. The chain is extra, but I'll give you a good deal.

CARLA: *(shaking her head, trying to be polite)* No...I don't think—

SLICK: Okay. The chain's included—but that deal's good only today.

CARLA: No. You see, I'm looking for something bigger than <u>that</u>.

SLICK: Gotcha! *(from behind the counter, he pulls out a huge, four- or five-foot garish, gaudy, glittery cross)* This is a <u>very</u> popular style, though of course it does run a bit more.

CARLA: Maybe you don't understand. I guess it's not the <u>size</u> of the cross as much as...Well, when my

friends became Christians, they carried big crosses, but they were rough, unpainted, plain wooden crosses. I thought they were crazy, but now I think I understand. Do you have anything in stock like that? Maybe this big? *(gestures size)*

SLICK: You know, I used to carry those, but they moved so slow that I discontinued that model. Hardly anyone wants to buy those. Most people just rent 'em—for those special occasions when you need to look the part, you see—and then return them.

CARLA: Can you tell me a store that <u>does</u> sell them?

SLICK: *(Pauses, considers **Carla** carefully while stroking his chin)* Well, I really shouldn't do this, but you look determined. I'll draw you a map. Here's where you can find them. *(he quickly sketches out a map on a scrap of paper)* It's called The Cross Shop, corner of Fifth and Main. The guy doesn't do much business, but he may have what you're looking for.

CARLA: Thanks! *(exits, passing two others entering the shop)*

SLICK: Hel-lo. Come in, come in. How can I help you today? *(lights out)*

SCENE 2

The Cross Shop. A counter behind which is a row of only one kind of cross—big wooden ones. A salesman is behind the counter.

SIMON: Hello. My name is Simon. Can I help you?

CARLA: My name is Carla and I just became a Christian. I'd like to buy a cross. *(looks at the display of crosses)* These are perfect...just what I've been looking for.

SIMON: Sure this is what you want?

CARLA: Positive. When I met Jesus, I was told that the cross of Christ would bring me tests and hardship as well as great joy. But I know that God will give me the strength I need and that he'll never leave me.

SIMON: Sounds like you're a determined young lady. This the one you want? *(**Carla** nods, and **Simon** hands her the cross)* There you go.

CARLA: How much do I owe you?

SIMON: Nothing.

CARLA: Nothing?

SIMON: Not right now, at least.

CARLA: But I was just at Crosses Galore, and Mr. Slick told me that—

SIMON: I know. Some people think they can buy their salvation like that. They're wrong. You begin paying when you carry it out the door.

CARLA: Thanks, Simon. By the way, how'd you ever get into this line of work?

SIMON: My family's been in this business a long time. An ancestor of mine—after whom I'm named—opened the first shop in Cyrene. His first cross was a lot like the one you have there. *(if biblical literacy is not your group's strong suit, at this point **Simon** may read Matthew 27:32: "As they were going out, they met a man from Cyrene, named Simon, and they forced him to carry the cross")* Now that you have your cross, I'd like to pass along something a missionary once said. His name was Jim Elliot. "He is no fool who gives what he cannot keep to gain what he cannot lose." Maybe that'll help you.

CARLA: *(thoughtfully)* Thanks, Simon. *(exits, lights out)*

SCENE 3

*School hallway, lockers in the background. Students are between classes. A group of three or four teenagers enter stage right, carrying books, chatting, laughing, etc., walk across stage and exit stage left—just as **Megan** and **Jenny** enter stage left.*

MEGAN: *(enthusiastically)* Isn't this exciting? Tomorrow is the last day of school!

JENNY: I can't wait. I'm gonna par-ty this summer. Hey, I like your top.

MEGAN: Thanks. I got it at the mall last night. Hey, did Dave call you last night? Karen told me he was going to—

*(Matt and **Tom** enter and interrupt)*

TOM: Hey, don't talk about the big party tonight without including us! What's happenin'?

MEGAN: Not much. Speaking of party animals *(she gives **Tom** a playful shove)*, did you hear that Carla became a Christian? I can't believe that someone who lived the way she did could be good enough to go to our church.

MATT: I heard that she's way too serious about it. One of my friends saw her at The Cross Shop. You wouldn't believe what she did. First Car—

TOM: *(interrupting)* Shhh! Here she comes. *(The group of teenagers all pretend to be doing something else)*

CARLA: *(enters with her big cross)* Hi, everyone. I guess you heard I became a Christian.

MEGAN: Yes, that's great! *(Megan's actual thought, spoken by an offstage voice, perhaps with a microphone)* I can't believe she's carrying that ugly cross.

TOM: We're really happy for you. *(Tom's actual thought, spoken by an offstage voice)* I've got to get out of here before everyone sees me with her and starts laughing.

MATT: You'll have to come to the next youth meeting at our church. *(spoken by an offstage voice)* I hope she decides to go to a different church.

JENNY: I heard the bad news about Brad. It must have been hard breaking up with him because he's not a Christian. *(spoken by an offstage voice)* Maybe he'll ask me out now.

CARLA: Yeah, it was hard. But it was the best way to go. I hope he'll become a Christian, too. Maybe you guys can witness to him.

ALL: Sure, sure. *(spoken by an offstage voice)* No way we could do that. We'd feel so stupid.

CARLA: Speaking of witnessing, where's your crosses? *(everyone reveals a tiny cross, worn in an inconspicuous place—except **Matt**, who keeps looking for his during the next few moments, and finally gives up looking)*

CARLA: They are nice...but isn't it hard for people to see them?

MEGAN: Well...maybe...but if people look hard enough they can see them fine.

TOM: Besides, we don't want people to get the wrong first impression.

MATT: When we first became Christians, we all had crosses like yours, Carla. But it was so hard to witness to our friends because those humongous crosses really irritated them. They finally avoided us—or laughed at us.

JENNY: Or both.

TOM: This way, if we don't want people to know that we're—I mean, we can share our faith when we want to...you know, when the time is right. *(Everyone but **Carla** nods in agreement. The bell rings and they all rush off, leaving **Carla** standing alone and looking puzzled. Lights out)*

SCENE 4

*A big sign in the background says "PARTY," with an arrow pointing offstage, stage right. A smaller sign reads "PARK YOUR CROSS, 50¢." **Matt, Tom, Megan,** and **Jenny** enter from stage left and go to center stage.*

TOM: *(To **Matt**)* Hey, your cross is showing.

MATT: Oh, thanks. I forgot all about it. *(puts his necklace inside his shirt)*

CARLA: *(approaching with her big cross)* Hi, guys!

MEGAN: Look, Carla, why don't you leave your cross outside before we go in to the party. It would look...uh, better that way.

CARLA: What do you mean?

MEGAN: Well, there might be some...uh, drinking, maybe, and stuff going on...

CARLA: You mean you guys are going to—

JENNY: We're just going to the party to have a good time. All our friends are there. That thing *(pointing to*

the cross) might bother some people. It will probably just get in the way of things. *(A teenager—with a cross just like Carla's—enters stage left, parks his cross under the "PARK YOUR CROSS" sign, then heads out stage right toward the party)*

TOM: It's not that hard to do, Carla. Think about it. *(all but Carla exit toward the party)*

CARLA: *(to herself, but aloud)* But <u>shouldn't</u> it be hard to do? *(lights out)*

SCENE 5

Next day, Mexican restaurant. Matt, Tom, Megan, and Jenny are sitting around a table waiting for the waitress to bring their lunch. Tom is playing with packages of hot sauce. Megan has a squirt gun.

MEGAN: Wasn't that a great party last night?

JENNY: It was super! *(To Matt)* Hey, what's wrong?

MEGAN: I think he's had too much hot sauce. This will cool him off! *(takes out her squirt gun and shoots him. Everyone laughs—except Matt)*

JENNY: What's wrong? Still worried you won't graduate? I heard Mr. Keller's final was really tough.

MATT: No, it's not that. I just...well, I'm thinking about going back to my old cross.

TOM: <u>What?</u> That big hunk of hardwood? C'mon, you've been studying too hard. I think your brain's burned out.

MATT: No, I'm serious. I've been thinking about it a lot lately.

MEGAN: You can't do this to us. We've got a great summer ahead of us—the <u>four</u> of us.

TOM: We haven't got room for that cross—and besides...oh, I get it. You'll only carry it to church and maybe to youth group, right?

MATT: No, I want it with me all the time. I know it'll get in the way, but I've gotta do it. I've been watching Carla the last couple of days. She reminds me of how things used to be with me. When I first became a Christian, I was proud to carry that cross around. I couldn't read my Bible enough, I couldn't wait to tell my friends about Jesus.

JENNY: But we've got our crosses. They're just more convenient than the big model, and they accomplish the same thing.

MATT: Do they? When was the last time someone noticed your cross, Jenny? When was the last time any of us explained to someone what the cross meant?

MEGAN: But Jesus never said the cross had to be big.

MATT: Yeah, but the cross Jesus carried and was crucified on wasn't gold-plated. You couldn't wear it around your neck. It was heavy and splintery. It caused him pain. It was work for him to carry it. I think it should be the same for us.

TOM: I think your brain is bummed out. *(The girls laugh and nod in agreement. Lights out)*

SCENE 6

School hallway, the next day. Matt, Tom, Megan, and Jenny enter stage right, talking. When Matt notices Carla entering stage left—carrying her big cross—he leaves the other three to talk with her. The three continue walking and exit stage left.

MATT: Carla! Am I glad to see you. I've got something to tell you.

CARLA: What is it?

MATT: *(takes a big breath)* I've decided to take up the cross I used to have when I first became a Christian.

CARLA: I don't understand.

MATT: You reminded me of the way I used to be when I first met Christ. Not ashamed of my faith, wherever I went, no matter who I was with. I want that again—thanks to you, Carla.

CARLA: I...I don't know what to say. I mean...I've been doing a lot of thinking. That's why I was late to first period today. I was wondering if it was even worth carrying this cross anymore. But I decided to stay with it.

MATT: Why?

CARLA: I remembered something that Simon—well, this guy I got my cross from, he told me something a missionary once said: "He is no fool who gives what he cannot keep to gain what he cannot lose."

MATT: I'm glad you didn't give up, Carla. *(bell rings)*

CARLA: See you Sunday at youth group?

MATT: Wouldn't miss it! *(begins walking away, but stops at Carla's next word)*

CARLA: Hey. *(pause)* I love you, brother.

MATT: Love you, too. *(The two hug, then exit. Lights out.)*

A voice offstage with a microphone reads Mark 8:34-38:

> Calling to the crowd to join his disciples, he said, "Anyone who intends to come with me has to let me lead. You're not in the driver's seat; <u>I</u> am. Don't run from suffering; embrace it. Follow me and I'll show you how. Self-help is no help at all. Self-sacrifice is the way, my way, to saving yourself, your true self. What good would it do to get everything you want and lose you, the real you? What could you ever trade your soul for?
>
> "If any of you are embarrassed over me and the way I'm leading you when you get around your fickle and unfocused friends, know that you'll be an even greater embarrassment to the Son of Man when he arrives in all the splendor of God, his Father, with an army of the holy angels.")

END

(Scripture passage from *The Message: The New Testament in Contemporary Language*, translated by Eugene H. Peterson, NavPress, 1993)

CHAPTER SEVEN

HOLIDAYS

ST. VALENTINE'S DAY
Valenteams

Need to divide your group quickly—but with some Valentines fun—into teams? Determine before your party how many teams you want, then pull that many sets of phrases out of several bags of conversation hearts (Cool Kid, Kiss Me, My Gal, etc.).

When kids walk into the party, give them each one heart to hold on to—not eat! When the time comes to make teams, tell everyone to find others with their phrase. They can yell back and forth as much as they want until they all team up.

To divide for another team game, have everyone with the same *color* heart get together. *Tommy Baker, Florence, Ky.*

Loves Me, Loves Me Not

Kick off your Valentine's Day
party—or your unit
on dat-

Though I went steady with someone my entire eighth-grade year, in high school I was always getting dumped. I never had a relationship that lasted more than two weeks. It seemed the people I was attracted to were never attracted to me; and the people that were interested in me, I had no interest in. Thus my love life in high school consisted of lots of dates but no steady. The same story continued on [col]lege until I met my spouse-to-be [...] than the [...]

ing and commitment—with this panel discussion.

Prior to your meeting ask four adults to each draft a short paragraph about their high school dating experiences, excluding any references that would identify them as male or female. Try to pick individuals that represent more than one kind of experience: married, unmarried, heavy high school daters, late bloomers who didn't date until college, a woman who married her high school sweetheart, a man who married his wife a month after their first date, etc. Photocopy these paragraphs without naming the writers.

At the party or meeting, hand out the copies to the kids—while the four writers are seated up front. Students have to guess which story goes with which individual.

After the "unveiling," kids jot down questions on an index card, directing them to a certain panel member, or to panel members of a certain gender, if they want. *Deborah Carlson and Robert Malsack, Brooklyn, Mich.*

LENT/EASTER
Recapture the King

This twist on Capture the Flag is an entertaining way to demonstrate the impossibility of stealing Jesus' body from a heavily guarded grave. So you should realize from the outset (though let your students discover this fact gradually) that it's virtually impossible for the Disciples to recapture the King. For that reason, let each game go only five to 15 minutes; Romans and Disciples should switch roles with every new game.

Play "Recapture the King" with anywhere from a dozen to 100 players. Choose a King and divide the rest of the group into Disciples and Romans (one Disciple for every three to five Romans). Lay out the borders of your playing field, and let the Romans pick out a holding place for the King. (It can be wherever they wish, as long as the hiding place has at least one entrance). The Romans must have a minimum of three guards around the holding place; there is no maximum. Designate also a safety zone for the Disciples and two jails: one for captured Disciples and one for captured Romans.

The object of this game is for the Disciples to recapture their King from the Romans—who are guarding him (or her) in a holding place—and to return him to the Disciples' safety zone. To start the game, the Romans send a messenger to the Disciples, telling them exactly where the King is being held. Then the Roman returns to his team and they all stay in one place, giving the Disciples a chance to hide.

Once play begins, the Romans start searching for the hidden Disciples, capturing them by tagging them with a touch. The captured Disciples are taken to jail. Disciples can also capture Romans—but only if *three* (or more) Disciples tag one at (or about) the same time. Both Romans and Disciples can be freed by being tagged by a member of their own team.

For the Disciples to recapture their King, at least two Disciples must escort him to the safety zone. For the Romans to win decisively, they must capture all the Disciples. If the Disciples haven't recaptured their King within that time—and the odds are tremendously against them—they lose. *Bill Fry, New Hartford, N.Y.*

Egg-Citing Egg Hunt

The object of this game is to accumulate the most plastic eggs within the time limit.

Each team of at least five teenagers chooses a spy from among them—then switch all the spies around into other teams so that no spy is with his or her original team. The spy in each team makes sure the team fulfills the instructions in one egg before finding another egg.

To prepare for the game, photocopy the list on page 45, or compose your own.

Insert each challenge in a plastic egg, then hide the eggs. If you want, play the game at night with flashlights. And put edible tidbits in each egg, along with the challenge.

When time is up, the spies must give the teams they've spied on a clean bill of health. The team with the most eggs wins. *James L Pagan, Orlando, Fla.*

Live from Jerusalem!

Presented as the talk show of a Jerusalem TV station, this 15-to-20-minute drama takes place shortly after Christ's resurrection. The single set is a talk-show set, cushioned chair for the host and perhaps a sofa for guests. It begins on page 46. *Steve Fortosis, Portland, Ore.*

44

CHALLENGES FOR EGG-CITING EGG HUNT

Photocopy this page, then cut apart the challenges and put one in each plastic egg.

Form a circle, facing inward. As a group, count to 40—the first person says "One," the teammate next to her says "Two," etc. When a team member comes to five or a multiple of five, he must clap instead of saying the number. If someone makes a mistake, the team must start the count over again.

Quickly choose a cheerleader to lead a simple cheer. Example: "Give me a B! Give me a U! Give me a N! Give me another N! Give me a Y! What does it spell? (BUNNY!) Can't hear you! (BUNNY!)"

The next egg you find must be green.

Find a tree. Circle it and sing "Ring around the Rosie" three times. And everyone *must* fall down.

Do the bunny hop to the next egg.

The next egg must be found by the youngest person in your group.

Make piggyback pairs to find the next egg.

Determine whose birthday is the nearest, and sing a raucous version of Happy Birthday to him or her.

Sit in a circle and do The Wave (you must stand up when it's your turn).

Build a pyramid and hold it for 10 seconds.

Spell EASTER by each of you contorting your body to shape a letter.

Live from Jerusalem!

Characters:

(in either Middle Eastern or modern costuming; the cast can be cut as needed)

Talk show host
Albert Rosenthal III (a Pharisee)
Lazarus

Mary (mother of Jesus)
Peter
Rashid (boy with the lunch)

Ben Goldberg (formerly blind)
Thomas
Pontius Pilate

Applause—either canned or live, prompted by "Applause" sign—as Shavitz walks onstage.

ANNOUNCER: *(unseen, over the sound system)* Live from Jerusalem, it's the Simeeeeeooooon Shavitz Show!

SHAVITZ: Hey, well, here we are again, sitting pretty here in Jerusalem, home of the blessed patriarchs and the not-so-blessed uniformed grunts that Caesar so kindly shipped over to us—hey, did I say that? Welcome anyway to a great lineup tonight.

We're broadcasting live from the Outer Courts up here on Temple Hill, and do we have a controversial lineup tonight! Ten days ago a rural laborer and sometime street preacher out of Nazareth was executed by the Romans. Shortly after his death came rumors that this Jesus of Nazareth was missing from his tomb. Stranger yet is the unsubstantiated report that he came alive again; in fact, some of his followers claim to have seen him, postdeath. We've gathered both supporters and skeptics tonight to interview—and just maybe we'll uncover the truth about this.

Welcome with me our first guest, the mother of yet one more in a long line of self-proclaimed, upcountry messiahs—Mary! *(applause)*

SHAVITZ: Evening, ma'am.

MARY: Good evening, Simeon.

SHAVITZ: How does it feel to know you raised a son who turned out to be such an incredibly controversial figure?

MARY: I didn't <u>teach</u> him to be controversial—it just happened because he is who he is.

SHAVITZ: And, uh, just who <u>is</u> he?

MARY: The Son of God.

SHAVITZ: Whoa, think ya lost me already. You saying that you, uh, got together somehow with, uh, the Man Upstairs, the Rabbi in the Sky, and, uh—

MARY: My husband's name was Joseph. But before we married, God gave me a son—<u>his</u> Son.

SHAVITZ: Sure, right, that clears everything up. *(nervous laughter)* Well, to move on...at any rate, I am sincerely sorry that your son had to die the way he did. Our imported wannabe tyrants have no business laying a hand on any Jew, be he God or fraud.

MARY: Well, thank you for your sympathy. I do think, though, that he wanted it to be clear that he died so that we could live.

SHAVITZ: *(stares at **Mary** without speaking for a moment, then rises and ushers her offstage)* Ooookay. Well, we've got a lot of guests waiting tonight, so we'll have to cut off our pleasant chat right here. Thanks for joining us, Mary. *(applause)* Next we have a man who says he used to be blind, but no more. Jesus, he claims, healed him. Welcome with me Ben Goldberg! *(applause as **Goldberg** walks on stage and seats himself)* So you say Jesus healed you.

GOLDBERG: Exactly.

SHAVITZ: How'd it all happen?

GOLDBERG: He spit on dirt and made a little mud. This is what my friends tell me—I couldn't see anything yet myself, of course. Then he smeared the dab of mud on my eyes and told me to wash it off in a pool.

SHAVITZ: Hey, my wife puts mud packs on her face, but I never knew one of those suckers could heal blindness! *(laughs)*

GOLDBERG: It can if Jesus applies it.

SHAVITZ: *(embarrassed pause)* We hear the

Pharisees threw you out of the synagogue for believing in this Jesus.

GOLDBERG: You heard right. And that's not the only thing jealousy drove them to.

SHAVITZ: Well, we'll let them answer for themselves, because our next guests are two of the leading Pharisees in the Sanhedrin. *(Ben rises to leave; applause)* Let's bring on the big boy now—welcome Pharisee Albert Rosenthal III! *Rosenthal enters; as he passes the exiting Shavitz, Rosenthal conspicuously walks widely around him. He is seated)*

SHAVITZ: So you weren't exactly bosom buddies with the naive Nazarene, huh?

ROSENTHAL: If you overlooked his heretical illusions of grandeur, his utopian teachings, and his deified death wish, you could probably get along with him okay.

SHAVITZ: Hey, you're forgetting what every Tom, Dick, and Harry on this end of the Mediterranean is talking about—his kindness, his miracles, his mercy.

ROSENTHAL: His kindness was only cunning, his miracles were merely magic, and his mercy only deceived the multitudes. Besides, the writings of the Prophets agree that the true Messiah will be born in Bethlehem. Jesus was from Nazareth. The Messiah will deliver us from our oppressors. Jesus went without a struggle to his own crucifixion. He couldn't fight his way out of a wet paper bag—not to mention a sealed granite tomb.

SHAVITZ: His followers say he's alive again.

ROSENTHAL: *(rolls his eyes and sighs loudly)* Another lie. His followers stole the body from the tomb and hid it.

SHAVITZ: You got some skeptics, Rosenthal. How did they get past the Roman guards, into a sealed tomb—you know as well as I do the size of a typical stone door—and out again, with the body, past the guards?

ROSENTHAL: Bribes, obviously.

SHAVITZ: Right, and we all know the millions of denari fishermen earn at their fragrant job. Well, thanks for being on the show, guy. *(applause as Rosenthal rises and leaves)* Speaking of fishermen, let's hope they left their occupational aroma at

home—because here are two of Jesus' actual disciples—Peter and Thomas! *(Applause as Rosenthal leaves and Peter and Thomas walk on. After hearing who's following him, Rosenthal just shakes his head as he leaves the stage)*

SHAVITZ: Well, Pete—or should I call you Rocky?—you seem awfully happy, considering you just lost your rabbi. In fact, what is this stolen-body scenario, anyway?

PETER: Hard to believe, I know. But believe me anyway: Jesus isn't dead. I've seen him myself.

SHAVITZ: Okey dokey, Pete—confession's good for the soul. What else did you see at that opium party?

THOMAS: I doubted it too, Simeon. But then I saw Jesus with my own eyes. I even touched his scars.

SHAVITZ: Well for the love of Osiris...you guys are making this Jesus out to be some kind of god. Gimme a break.

PETER: If we hadn't been so dense at the time, we would have heard Jesus say himself that he'd be killed and then come back to life. Alive enough, in fact, to help break a week-long fishing slump that had put me behind on my mortgage. I'm caught up now, thanks to him.

SHAVITZ: So you're still fishing instead of hitting the speaking circuit? You know, "Disciple of Judean Messiah Tells You How to Stretch Your Loaves and Fishes"?

PETER: Fishing, but not the kind you have in mind.

SHAVITZ: Well, guys, gotta move on—but why don't you stick around? You know the next guy we're bringin' on. Come on in, Lazarus! *(Applause as Lazarus enters)*

SHAVITZ: We couldn't talk about a resurrection without talking with a recognized expert on the subject. Lazarus says <u>he</u> rose from the dead, too! You're one of a select few, Laz. Does this mean you're the Son of God, too?

LAZARUS: Heck, no. The difference is, I was a goner. There was no way I could have revived myself. If Jesus hadn't come along, I'd still be pushing up lilies. Jesus raised <u>himself</u> from the dead—by his own power—which I couldn't have

done.

SHAVITZ: And the source of his power?...

LAZARUS: He's the Son of God, so he's got all of God's power.

SHAVITZ: *(leaning forward, looking hard at Lazarus, and momentarily getting serious)* You actually believe this guy is God?

LAZARUS: Yup. Proved it by his miracles, his perfect life, his teachings, his resurrection—

SHAVITZ: Hold on a minute. How did his resurrection prove he was God?

LAZARUS: If he was just a man, like you or me, he'd still be dead.

SHAVITZ: Whoa! It's getting a little thick in here. *(laughs nervously)* Anyway, we've got someone who may be Jesus' youngest follower waiting to come on. Welcome Rashid—the boy with the lunchbox.

(Applause as young Rashid joins the others onstage)

SHAVITZ: So you're the boy who gave his lunch to Jesus.

RASHID: Huh-huh.

SHAVITZ: What happened? The Twelve ran out of peanut butter and jelly, and you came to the rescue?

RASHID: Jesus didn't have any food for this big crowd, so I gave him my lunch.

SHAVITZ: Exactly how big <u>was</u> this crowd?

RASHID: The grownups said there were more than 5,000 people.

SHAVITZ: I've heard about boys with hollow legs, but this is ridiculous. What does your mom give you for lunch, Meals on Wheels?

RASHID: All I had was five loaves of bread and two fish.

SHAVITZ: Jesus must have sliced that bread pretty thin, huh?

RASHID: Oh no, everybody was stuffed. In fact, they picked up a bunch of leftovers afterwards.

SHAVITZ: Well, kid, you're either one of the best little liars around, or this Jesus was a first-rate magician. Hey, I want to thank you and Laz here for appearing on the show. *(applause)* Our last guest is Caesar's toady in these parts—the man who couldn't bring himself to give a decisive sentence against Jesus, so he just washed his hands of the whole deal and let the mob goad the soldiers into doing the

dirty work. Sounds like a Roman to me. Hey, why doesn't this guy wash his hands of Judea itself and go home already? Just kidding. Let's give Pontius Pilate a big welcome.

*(Applause as the other guests leave and **Pilate** enters)*

PILATE: Watch it, Shavitz. Keep running at the mouth like that, and I'll have you arrested for treason. My personal guard is outside your studio doors at this moment.

SHAVITZ: Ratings, Governor Pilate, just ratings. No harm meant. Were you satisfied with the outcome of the Jesus scandal?

PILATE: *(getting comfortable, crossing his legs)* I'll tell you one thing: I've taken a cartload of sleeping pills since that crucifixion. I can't get the guy out of my mind. He still plagues me night and day.

SHAVITZ: Guilt, I suppose.

PILATE: Well, yeah, I do feel guilty—but there's nothing I can do about it now. Just the night before he was brought to trial, my wife had a terrible nightmare about the man and warned me to leave him alone. But I had to do what I did...I couldn't risk a full-scale riot.

SHAVITZ: We're almost out of time, governor. One last question: Do you put any credence in the rumor that Jesus has come back to life?

PILATE: *(pensive and troubled, almost as if talking to himself)* I don't know...Sometimes I think almost anything's possible with this man...I can still see him looking at me, still hear him saying that I have no real authority...I can't forget him. I just can't forget the man. *(bows his head and covers his face with his hands. Blackout)*

OFFSTAGE VOICE: I am the resurrection and the life; whoever believeth in me, though he were dead, yet shall he live. And whosoever liveth and believeth in me shall never die.

CHAPTER EIGHT

CAMPS & RETREATS

Cleanup Deposit

If your church owns or rents a vehicle for youth trips, you know how fast trash can accumulate in it. Usually the youth minister or leader gets stuck cleaning it up.

Why not consider a "Cleanup Deposit" for your next trip? Before the trip ask for five dollars (or whatever amount you choose) as a deposit to ensure a clean bus or van. *Everyone* forfeits their deposit if the vehicle is trashy—yes, even if it's not their trash. *Greg Miller, Knoxville, Tenn.*

Stuffed Animals

Fifth and sixth graders are often anxious about being away from home for an entire week of summer camp. To help alleviate their anxiety, make it mandatory for them to bring their favorite stuffed animal to camp. (Many want to anyway!)

When campers arrive, their stuffed animals are immediately turned over to a designated counselor.

The counselor privately takes all fuzzy friends to a room where each animal is given an award—fuzziest, most loveable, cuddliest, brightest eyes, most love-worn, most adorable, most huggable, snuggliest, strangest, etc.

After the evening meal that night, set all the stuffed animals out in the meeting room. Hold up each one while reading off its award, and then have the kids guess who it belongs to. Throughout the week the young people will proudly and gladly sleep with their stuffed animals because everyone has one. (For a different kind of stuffed-animal meeting for high schoolers, see page 33.) *Carolyn Peters, Beaver Dam, Wis.*

Go Ahead and Leaf

Sometime during your next camping trip or retreat weekend, send teens out for a nature walk. Ask them to look around and find a leaf that describes them to other people. When the teens return, have them explain why they picked their leaf. Read some Bible verses that talk about leaves (for example, Prov. 11:28 and Psa. 1:1-3).

This simple activity can cover a host of themes including obedience, self-image, and similarities and differences as a family. *Laura Weller, Boyertown, Pa.*

Star Search

Want an unusual but effective segue into a talk or devotional during your next camping trip or night hike? If you'll be far enough away from the city to have really dark night skies, take along copies of

pages 51-52 for everyone, and spend a few minutes during the day pointing out the most obvious constellations as they appear on the sheet. You may want different students to memorize the shape of different constellations.

That night, find a site away from lights—a field, a hilltop, even a dark parking lot works—as long as your view of the sky is as large as possible from horizon to horizon.

If you take the star-chart sheets with you, tape red cellophane over the flashlight heads so that the frequent flicking on of the white lights doesn't kill everyone's night vision. (You can get adhesive red cellophane at auto parts shops.) Now let kids find their constellations—and watch for the slow-moving satellites within an hour or two of sunset, and for meteors ("shooting stars") that zip across a corner of the sky.

Many of the constellations reflect biblical characters (Virgo the Virgin suggests Mary, Leo the Lion suggests either Christ or the lion Samson killed), events (Gemini the Twins suggests the birth and lives of Jacob and Esau, the Northern Cross or Cygnus suggests the Crucifixion, Cetus the Whale suggests Jonah's misadventure), and themes (Bootes the Shepherd suggests Christ, Draco the Dragon and Scorpius the Scorpion suggest Satan). Come with a little preparation, and give your talk right out there under the stars, as you connect the constellations and the stories behind them with biblical truths. *Doug Partin, Artesia, N.Mex.*

The Night Sky

Constellation names in all capital letters; other names are star names.

SPRING

NORTH

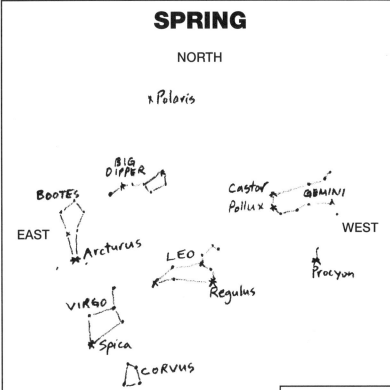

EAST

WEST

SOUTH

Spring

• The handle of the **Big Dipper** "arcs to **Arcturus**."
• A line extended through the Big Dipper's front two "pointer stars" takes you north to **Polaris**, the North Star, and the other way to **LEO the Lion**.
• The head of **LEO the Lion** is a big backwards question mark, with Leo's brightest star, **Regulus**, at the bottom of the question mark.

Summer

• At the corners of the "Summer Triangle" are the bright stars **Deneb**, **Vega**, and **Altair** (in **CYGNUS the Swan**, **LYRA the Lyre**, and **AQUILA the Eagle**, respectively).
• **CYGNUS the Swan** is also called the Northern Cross. The Swan flies south along the Milky Way.

SUMMER

NORTH

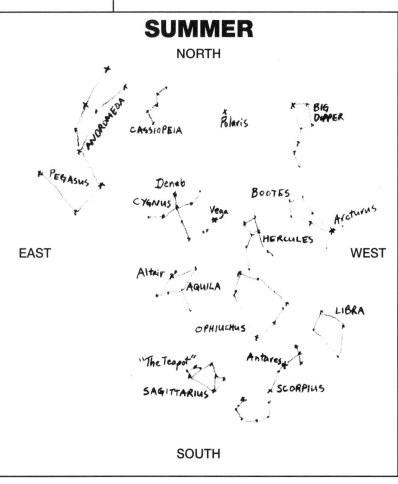

EAST

WEST

SOUTH

51

The Night Sky (cont'd.)

AUTUMN

NORTH

(star chart showing:) BIG DIPPER, Polaris, AURIGA, Capella, CASSIOPEIA "The W", Vega, Deneb, PERSEUS, TAURUS, ANDROMEDA, WEST, EAST, Aldebaran, Pleiades, ARIES, PEGASUS, Altair, "The Square", CETUS, Formalhaut

SOUTH

Autumn

• High overhead is **CASSIOPEIA the Queen**, a "W" pattern of stars (some see an upside-down "M").
• The Great Square in the south is **PEGASUS the Flying Horse**.
• **CETUS the Whale** is in the south.
• **PERSEUS** is the hero who rescued **ANDROMEDA**, the daughter of **CASSIOPEIA the Queen**.

Winter

• **ORION the Hunter**: The three closely spaced stars across the middle of **ORION** is his belt. A straight line drawn through the belt and extended to the right (and curved a little upward) brings you to **ALDEBARAN**, the reddish eye of **TAURUS the Bull**. Extended to the left, the line takes you to **SIRIUS**.
• **SIRIUS**: The "Dog Star," so named because it is the brightest star in **Canus Major**, the "Big Dog" of the hunter Orion. **SIRIUS** is also the brightest star in the night sky.
• **PLEIADES**: A tiny "dipper" of six jewel-like stars, to the northwest of **Aldebaran**.

WINTER

NORTH

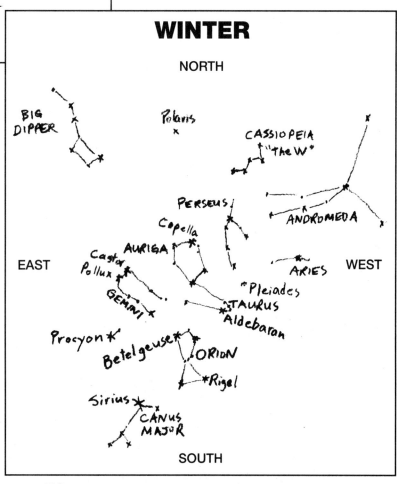

(star chart showing:) BIG DIPPER, Polaris, CASSIOPEIA "the W", PERSEUS, ANDROMEDA, Copella, AURIGA, EAST, Castor, Pollux, GEMINI, ARIES, WEST, Pleiades, TAURUS, Aldebaran, Procyon, Betelgeuse, ORION, Rigel, Sirius, CANUS MAJOR

SOUTH

52

CHAPTER NINE

SERVICE PROJECTS

Get-Well Video

Is a member of your group in the hospital or facing a lengthy recuperation at home? Schedule an ice-cream party in her honor and videotape the kids and adults who attend. Videotape students doing goofy things, and give everyone a chance to send messages via the tape. A small group of close friends can deliver the tape.

This easy, inexpensive, and entertaining project tells kids that you love them, you're praying for them, and you care. Adapt it to encourage those who are off to college and struggling with loneliness. *Mark A. Simone, Chagrin Falls, Ohio*

F.A.I.T.H. Projects

Sometimes service projects come across as dreary duties with no connection to a personal faith in Christ. Why settle for mere service projects when you can offer F.A.I.T.H. projects: *Faith Acting In Teens' Hands.* Tie every project directly to biblical faith and our responsibility to help others as representatives of Jesus.

With F.A.I.T.H. projects, teens find a new sense of confidence in their commitment to Christ as they learn to support others. Cleaning houses, mowing lawns, or washing cars takes on new meaning when they are seen as spiritual disciplines. Serving at social functions by waiting tables, washing dishes, or mopping floors become holy activities as kids see their hands as extensions of Jesus' hands.

Frightening tasks like working with the elderly or sick become easier when young people realize they are not alone with their challenge, but that God is at work in them. Adult responsibilities like the care of young children or the supervision of older children are seen as opportunities to learn patience under the influence of the Holy Spirit. These are also sacrificial acts that show Christlike mercy to parents who are relieved of their responsibilities for a time.

An even more substantial sacrifice: use youth group funds to send those same parents out for the evening at a cozy restaurant, then to a bed and breakfast.

Challenge your group to be involved in F.A.I.T.H. projects on a regular basis (one every two months is realistic).

To get the most from F.A.I.T.H. projects, recruit leaders for this ministry rather than asking for volunteers. Some can be entirely youth led; other projects need adult supervision. Invest time in your leaders to help them understand the larger spiritual meaning of a project and then ask them to contact teens personally to serve. *Bryan Carpenter and Tommy Baker, Florence, Ky.*

CHAPTER TEN

PUBLICITY

Color Posters

Tired of plain old black and white? It only requires a little work on your part to turn your copy machine into a color copier.

Create a clip-art poster or similar artwork to a point that it can be photocopied cleanly. If you plan

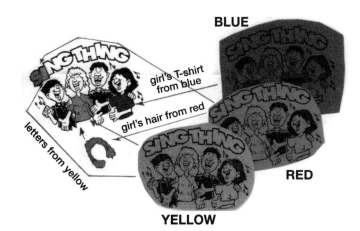

BLUE

girl's T-shirt from blue

girl's hair from red

letters from yellow

RED

YELLOW

to color your letters, they will have to be outline style. (Solid letters will be black no matter what.)

Copy the poster onto several different colored sheets (construction paper will work on a machine with a hand feeder). Use one copy of whichever color you wish your background to be as the master poster.

Cut out parts of the subjects from the colored copies and glue them in place on the master poster (cut a person's hair out of brown paper, pieces of clothing out of red, and so on).

If you plan to display permanent posters (door signs, etc.), you may wish to seal them in plastic covers. *Len Cuthbert, Hamilton, Ont., Canada*

Roundball Round-Up

Meet your kids at church on a Saturday afternoon, and bring as many basketballs as possible. Divide into teams and disperse around town. Have teams go to schools, apartment complexes, parks—wherever there are hoops—and begin playing basketball. As other teens and children pass by, invite them to join the game. Introduce yourselves, get to know the kids, and invite them to church. *John Peters, Cleveland, Tenn.*

Video Awards

Create a nonthreatening way for kids to not only invite their friends to events, but to prove to them that the activities are actually fun. Recruit a volunteer video photographer for every event to tape the highlights. Kick off the activities by announcing that the most enthusiastic participant of the evening will receive an award at the end of the event. Give the winner a certificate or button as well as the videotape of the night's events. *Len Cuthbert, Hamilton, Ont., Canada*

Welcome Postcards

Inundate incoming kids with welcoming mail around promotion time.

1. Shortly before promotion, scan the Sunday school lists for names and addresses of youths graduating into your group.

2. Ask for 30 volunteers from your youth group to address postcards. Each new member's name and address should show up on 30 cards.

3. While the group is addressing postcards, brainstorm 30 topics relating to the youth group—activities, studies, food, games, service projects, singing, etc.

4. Assign each volunteer one of the topics, and give that volunteer one set of preaddressed cards. If there are 14 incoming youths, for instance, each volunteer receives one card addressed to each of the 14—or 14 cards total. The volunteers then write a brief note to each new kid about an assigned topics. (Veteran members can assist newer members with necessary information.) All cards must be turned in to the church office within the week.

5. About a week before the incoming kids start attending youth group, begin a daily mail campaign using the prewritten postcards. Stamp and mail a topical set of cards every day for 30 straight mailing days. The new members receiving daily postcards from peers in the group attend youth meeting with excitement and enthusiasm.

Jeff Elliott, Cleveland, Tenn.

Youth Calling Cards

As a visual reminder of who's missing, make up index cards for every youth involved in your program, complete with addresses, phone numbers, and any other helpful information (school activities, work location, and so on). Make up cards for youth prospects.

Print each teen's name in large letters at the top or on the back of the index card, and then tack all of the cards onto a bulletin board, using push pins. Label this board "Missing in Action," and mount it on the wall or the door of the meeting room. (Consider making multiple copies of the cards in case some are lost.)

Instruct the youths who attend the meetings to transfer their cards to an adjacent bulletin board labeled "Here and Now." It should be easy to see now who's missing from your meeting. Hand the "Missing in Action" cards to kids and youth leaders as a reminder to call or send a note to the missing students, or ask them to choose a card. They must return the card at the next meeting. Ask people not to take the same missing person's card two weeks in a row.

Before the next meeting, return the "Here and Now" cards to the "Missing in Action" board so that you're ready to use them again. *Greg Miller, Knoxville, Tenn.*

Dorky Cards

Is your church blessed with a stash of dorky greeting cards from the '40s and '50s that any self-respecting pastor would be utterly embarrassed to send out? Well they're just stupid enough to work as cards to junior or senior high students.

Send sympathy cards to kids on vacation or who are having the time of their lives at church camp. Get-well cards can be used for students who have achieved stellar success in athletics or academics.

Mike Evans, Portage, Mich.
